TWAYNE'S
RULERS AND STATESMEN OF THE WORLD
SERIES

Hans L. Trefousse, Brooklyn College
General Editor

JOSEPH STALIN

(TROW 10)

Joseph Stalin

By ROBERT D. WARTH

University of Kentucky

Twayne Publishers, Inc.   ::   New York

Preface

WHATEVER ONE MAY THINK OF STALIN AND STALINISM, IT IS HARDLY
necessary to argue that the man and his system has had—and
continues to have—a major role in shaping the history of the
Soviet Union and, indeed, twentieth-century civilization. It is
less evident that another study of the Soviet dictator serves a
useful purpose. But, oddly enough, both Russian and Western
scholars have shied away in recent years from a serious biography,
though of course for different reasons. I have attempted, therefore,
to supply a long-felt need within the modest scope of the present
series. In no sense does it claim to be definitive or to tap hitherto-
undisclosed sources of information. It does, however, have the
advantage of greater perspective and the use of primary materials
unavailable to previous biographers. For details, the reader is
referred to the bibliographical essay at the end of the book.

Stalin is dead, but Stalinism—however muted—lives on. Since
even the most prescient historian is unable to predict the future
with confidence, there is an unavoidable weakness in any biography of Stalin which seeks—as this one does—to trace Stalin's
legacy in the Soviet Union and in the contemporary world. The
Russian invasion of Czechoslovakia in the summer of 1968, which
occurred after the text was completed, has given rise to speculation that it presages a return to Stalinism in the Soviet Union
and its satellite empire. So far, a significant revival of the Stalin
cult (as distinct from his brutal methods) has failed to materialize.
The cautious optimism that I ventured to express in the conclud-
ing chapter about a future turn toward Marxist social democracy
may seem misplaced. But a revision in the light of current events,
while momentarily tempting, is to slight the "long view" which
historians above all should cultivate. The successors of Kosygin
and Brezhnev will not be Stalin's henchmen, and a rehabilitation
of the old tyrant and his scheme of government furnishes no permanent base for political stability in a society that is changing
as rapidly as that of the Soviet Union.

Lexington, Kentucky   ROBERT D. WARTH
November 29, 1968

Contents

Chronology

1879 Born in Gori, Georgia.
1888 Begins formal education at the local church school.
1894 Enrolls at Tiflis Theological Seminary.
1898 Joins Georgian organization of socialists.
1900 Employed as clerk at Tiflis Geophysical Observatory.
1902 Arrested in Batum for revolutionary activity.
1903 Escapes from exile.
1903 Marries Catherine Svanidze.
1905 Attends Bolshevik conference at Tammerfors, Finland.
1907 Attends Russian Social Democratic party congress in London.
1908 Arrested in Baku and exiled.
1909– Escapes and is rearrested.
1910
1912 Becomes member of Bolshevik Central Committee.
1913 Publishes "Marxism and the National Question."
1913– Exiled to northern Siberia.
1917
1917 Arrives in Petrograd after February Revolution and assumes editorship of *Pravda*.
1917 Appointed Commissar for Nationality Affairs after October Revolution.
1919 Appointed a member of the Politburo, the highest party organ.
1919 Marries Nadezhda Alliluyeva.
1922 Appointed general secretary of the Communist party.
1924 Delivers eulogy at Lenin's funeral ("Stalin's oath").
1925– Ousts rivals from party leadership and consolidates dictatorship.
1927
1928 Inaugurates first Five Year Plan to industrialize Russia.
1929 Begins program to collectivize agriculture.
1932 Offers resignation as general secretary after Nadezhda Alliluyeva's suicide.
1934 Begins Great Purge following assassination of Sergei Kirov.

1936– Eliminates Old Bolsheviks at Moscow Trials.
1938
1939 Signs treaty of friendship and non-aggression with Nazi Germany.
1941 Becomes premier shortly before German invasion.
1943 Meets Roosevelt and Churchill at Teheran Conference.
1945 Confers with Roosevelt and Churchill at Yalta.
1945 Assumes title of generalissimo to celebrate victory over Germany.
1946 Replies to Churchill's "Iron Curtain" speech.
1947 Rebuffs Marshall Plan aid.
1948 Breaks with President Tito of Yugoslavia.
1949 Celebrates seventieth birthday.
1950 Publishes "Marxism and the Problem of Linguistics" on the Marr controversy.
1952 Publishes "Economic Problems of the U.S.S.R."
1952 Reorganizes party organs and prepares new purge.
1953 Dies at his dacha near Moscow.

CHAPTER I

The Dictator

ON DECEMBER 21, 1929, JOSEPH STALIN, THE GENERAL SECRETARY of the Communist party of the Union of Soviet Socialist Republics, celebrated his fiftieth birthday. Such anniversaries are normally ceremonial rather than historical events, but on this occasion the ecstatic dithyrambs of the Soviet press honoring the "man of steel," "granite Bolshevik," and "iron Leninist" signaled a new and exalted status for the supposedly humble Georgian disciple of Marx and Lenin. He replied graciously and with becoming humility to these accolades, though he closed on an oddly sanguine note: "Your congratulations and greetings I place to the credit of the great Party of the working class which bore me and reared me in its own image and likeness. And just because I place them to the credit of our glorious Leninist Party, I make bold to tender you my Bolshevik thanks. You need have no doubts, comrades, that I am prepared in the future, too, to devote to the cause of the working class, to the cause of the proletarian revolution and world communism, all my strength, all my ability and, if need be, all my blood, drop by drop." [1]

The outside world had by then "discovered" Stalin. He was just becoming a figure of international renown, however, and press reports habitually referred to him as an "enigma," a "sphinx," and a man of mystery. During the early twenties he had been virtually unknown either in or out of Russia except to the political cognoscenti. The brilliant and flamboyant Leon Trotsky had shared the headlines with Lenin until the latter's lingering illness and death, and the defeat and ignominious exile of the "popular" favorite by a seemingly obscure party ward heeler was a baffling denouement even to experienced Kremlinologists.

During Stalin's hegemony of roughly a quarter century, in which the realities of his absolute power were never officially acknowledged, Stalin retained the image of a faithful and dedicated servant of the party. Actually he subjected the party, as he did every aspect of government and society, to a traumatic shock that significantly altered the nature of Bolshevism and the Soviet Union. Russia, in a word, became thoroughly Stalinized.

Stalin's rise to power was neither sudden nor spectacular. It lacked the precision and drama of a well executed coup d'état; it furnished no climax to a career of military glory; it evoked no response among the masses that testified to the charismatic spell of a master politician, skilled in the diagnosis of social pathology; and it produced no evidence by tongue or pen that the state had succumbed to the blandishments of a clever but shallow demagogue. Yet it was a classic performance in the art of political manipulation. The rival aspirants had been outmaneuvered at every turn, and their chagrin was expressed in outrage and bewilderment that an apparent nonentity had seized the ultimate prize. The neophyte dictator of 1929 was not the tyrant of the mid-thirties, crushing his "enemies" with ferocious severity. He was outwardly a modest man—taciturn, patient, and unpretentious. Certainly he was devoid of those obvious marks of showmanship and personal vanity so often associated with individuals in the public domain.

Stalin, to use the cliché of journalism, was colorless. His appearance added to the general impression of mediocrity, although official portraits and other examples of iconography contrived to invest both face and figure with grace and dignity. His complexion, rather swarthy as a young man, had grown sallow, and his face was marred by pockmarks and irregular blackened teeth with gold fillings. Abundant black hair and a bushy mustache, both beginning to gray during the 1930's, were his most striking features. Short, compact, and somewhat low slung, he was about 5'4" tall and inclined toward paunchiness in his middle years. Sensitive about his height, he permitted no one conspicuously taller than he in the inner councils of the party; and rumors persisted that he wore specially constructed shoes for added stature. His dress, like his manner, was simple: a plain khaki tunic buttoned to the neck and black leather boots sufficed on almost every occasion, whether public or private. He acquired a squirrel and reindeer overcoat shortly after the October Revolution and wore it with a fur cap for the rest of his life. During World War II, befitting his military rank, he wore a well tailored marshal's uniform for formal appearances. Spurning an array of medals and ribbons, he permitted himself a single decoration—the gold star representing the Order of Hero of the Soviet Union.

Opinions differ as to Stalin's personality, much less so about his character. With few exceptions, only court historians and political retainers have commented favorably upon the latter, and of course the record speaks for itself regarding the callous barbarism of his regime. It has been maintained with some plausibility that it was the system not the man that was faulty: "All-powerful as he was, he was impotent in the face of the frightful system that had grown up around him like a huge honeycomb, and he was help-less either to destroy it or bring it under control." [2] Lest one be tempted to commiserate with a dictator trapped by the bureau-cratic excrescences of his own dictatorship, one must recall that it was Stalin who originally fashioned the grand design. As frustrat-ing as he may have found his handiwork, there is no evidence that he ever considered altering the basic structure or, indeed, that he consciously recognized any serious flaws in the finished product.

For all his calculated brutality and vengeful suspiciousness, there is ample testimony that Stalin could exude a certain charm when he chose to do so. Nor was he lacking a sense of humor. Not all would agree that "his brown eye . . . [was] exceedingly kindly and gentle" or that "a child would like to sit in his lap and a dog would sidle up to him." [3] Others spoke of his eyes as "cold," "crafty," or like "chilled steel" and his smile as "man-aged." But he was hospitable and cordial to foreign guests, and among his cronies he could play the role of genial host without apparent affectation. His chief means of relaxation were lengthy dinners, replete with his favorite Georgian foods and wines, in which bantering small talk often concealed a serious undercur-rent of political discussion. Like most top party officials, he kept late hours, usually sleeping until mid-day and working after-noons and evenings. Foreigners seldom observed the unpleasant side of his personality, for he could be crude, irritable, and cal-lous. He is said to have sometimes referred to himself, half-apologetically, as "a rude old man." [4]

Stalin's natural habits and style of life were almost as austere as his manner and dress, but eventually he accepted the full pano-ply of bodyguards, cooks, housekeepers, and other servants in his Kremlin apartment and at his country estates. His dachas, aside from ample food and drink, were his one luxury. His favorite was at Kuntsevo just outside Moscow, built in 1934, where he was to die almost twenty years later. There were two more near Moscow and still others in the Black Sea area for summer vacations. Ex-cept for the war years he usually spent his nights at Kuntsevo, sleeping on a sofa and eating his meals (when there were no guests) at one end of a dining table piled high with newspapers and official documents. The acquisition of material goods did not attract him, and since his everyday needs were provided by the state the money from his salary simply piled up on his desk.

Stalin's chief factotum was Nikolai Vlasik, who had been originally assigned by the Red Army as a bodyguard during the civil war and rose to become chief of Stalin's personal security force with the rank of general. Described as "incredibly stupid, illiterate and uncouth," he nevertheless assumed the status of a petty tyrant because of his proximity to the ultimate source of all power in the Soviet Union. By the mid-thirties he not only supervised all of Stalin's residences but took it upon himself to interpret "the Boss's" tastes in such diverse matters as state banquets, movies, operas, and architecture.[5]

One facet of Stalin's complex personality impressed almost all observers aside from political opponents: his innate ability coupled with strength of leadership and tenacity of will. Stolid and pedestrian though he was, he conveyed an aura of controlled power and assured judgment. What he lacked in intellectual precocity—he was never a thinker in any original sense—was generously compensated by shrewd perspicacity and breadth of technical knowledge. He had little aptitude for self-analysis or self-doubt, usually an asset for politicians in general and dictators in particular. Whereas the ordinary man may fail to grasp the intracacies of a problem and the brilliant man may vacillate because of too complete an understanding, the true leader plunges onward in the expectation that the result will vindicate his action. Stalin possessed this quality of serene self-confidence in overabundance, and in the absence of constitutional safeguards or other checks to his personal authority, he was encouraged to think of himself as infallible. But he was by no means a reckless gambler. At times, particularly in the realm of foreign affairs, he was the epitome of cautious conservatism, unwilling to jeopardize the safety of the state for the possibility of national or ideological gain. Although he made grievous errors that would have terminated his career in a democratic country, he knew how to retreat gracefully when he had pushed his power to the limit. His mental aberrations were never so disabling that he became an emotional cripple, incapable of making rational decisions; nor, at another extreme, did his lust for power find expression in megalomania, a disorder for which dictators may be said to have an occupational propensity.

The buffetings of his childhood, the rigors of an underground existence, the recurrent ordeal of prison and exile, and the ten-sions of internecine political struggle all helped to temper the mature Stalin. His extraordinary insensitivity and coolness of nerve suggest an emotional block that prevented the give and take of normal human relationships. In all probability, to use the catchall phrase of psychiatry, he was a psychopathic personality. Yet the act of labeling, even when accurate, does not provide a diagnosis, and the clues that we possess as to the state of his psyche are too insubstantial for a psychological biography. It seems evident, however, that his adjustment to reality became more tenuous as his political authority increased. In Stalin's case, the power he wielded not only corrupted him; it made him a desperately sick and lonely man.

CHAPTER II

The Professional Revolutionary

YOSIF (JOSEPH) VISSARIONOVICH DJUGASHVILI—THE FUTURE STALIN
—was a native of Gori, Georgia, a picturesque mountain community of some 6,000 inhabitants at the time of his birth in 1879.
The ancient Caucasian kingdom of Georgia, once the center of a
flourishing civilization, had become a Russian protectorate late
in the eighteenth century and was annexed as part of the empire
in 1801.

Little is known of Stalin's early life, and even that must be
pieced together from fragmentary and contradictory evidence. Joseph—or Soso, the Georgian equivalent of Joe—was the fourth
child of Vissarion and Catherine Djugashvili, a young couple of
peasant background. His brothers had died in infancy, and as an
only child he received the devoted care of a patient and affectionate mother. His father, a shoemaker by trade, died when the boy
was only eleven. Yet if the traditional portrayal of the elder Djugashvili can be believed—that he was a drunken improvident
who beat his son with senseless cruelty—the time was sufficient to
mold Soso's personality toward that cold and ruthless pattern familiar in the mature Stalin. The hypothesis of a brutalized childhood can only partially illuminate the character of the future
dictator, but it does provide a psychological framework for an
otherwise dehumanized and abstract portrait.

Other misfortunes befell young Soso. At the age of seven, small-
pox left its indelible imprint on his face. A second and more critical illness developed from an infected arm, and Stalin later specu-
lated that he was perhaps saved by a "strong constitution or the
ointment of a village quack." [1] He retained a permanent handicap from the ordeal: his left arm could not be fully bent at the
elbow and was several inches shorter than the right. In 1916 he
was excused from military service because of the disability.

Catherine Djugashvili, who absorbed the piety common to one
of her sex and humble station in life, sent her son to the local
church school. Soso's formal education began in the autumn of
1888, several months before his ninth birthday. He proved a

bright and studious pupil during his six years at the Gori school, but it is doubtful that one so young, no matter how precocious, could have absorbed the rudiments of Marxism or become an atheist from reading Darwin. At any rate, this was the orthodox legend fashioned in Stalin's lifetime.

In September 1894 Soso enrolled in the theological seminary in Tiflis (now Tbilisi), the capital of Georgia and the metropolitan center of the Transcaucasus. A scholarship, obtained by the recommendations of his school principal and the local priest, provided for his basic expenses and testifies to his academic excellence and exemplary deportment. If the young Stalin was already a rebel, as his Soviet biographers imply, he disguised his feelings with exceptional skill.

The students led a semi-monastic existence, a monotonous round of prayers, classes, and study. The intellectual atmosphere was stifling—a compound of scholastic theology, rote learning, and Russian patriotism. This forced feeding of Orthodox piety led only to sullen resentment, and many who had begun their studies with a genuine calling for the priesthood were quickly disillusioned. Yet in an educationally impoverished land—Georgia had no college or university—the seminary was, if not a beacon of learning, a center of ideological ferment. Its graduates and former students constituted a substantial portion of the local intelligentsia, and they also nourished the now somewhat diminished flame of Georgian nationalism. Patriotic outbursts had for years been a frequent source of trouble to the seminary authorities. In 1886 the rector had been assassinated by a pupil expelled for anti-Russian sentiments, and the year before Soso's matriculation a strike, leading to the expulsion of eighty-seven offenders, caused the police to close the school for a time.

Soso shared the romantic nationalism of his classmates; and as in the case of so many ex-seminarians who were to play a role of consequence in the Social Democratic movement—Sylvester Djibladze, Noah Jordania, and Nikolai Chkheidze—nationalism led to a more searching probe of the social order. He read voraciously from the forbidden books that were smuggled in, chiefly literary classics and works on social problems, and his first year was one of rapid development toward intellectual maturity and political awareness. In 1895, according to the official chronology, he established contact with "underground groups of Russian revolutionary Marxists who had been exiled to Transcaucasia by the tsarist government." [2] The date is suspiciously early, though it is likely that he had some acquaintance with socialist theory. Marx's

Capital, however, was not widely available in Russian translation and was then unobtainable in Tiflis.

Stalin's active revolutionary career began in August 1898 when he joined a small organization of socialists in Tiflis, the so-called *Messameh Dassy* or "Third Group" (to distinguish it from two earlier political circles). Still a student at the seminary, he contrived to lead a double life while receiving instruction in practical work from his more seasoned comrades. Later, when he was assigned to lecture on Marxism to small groups of workmen, his simple speech and homely manner established a rapport with his audience that a more polished and sophisticated party worker might well have envied. This insight into the pragmatic world of the ordinary man seems to have been a natural gift, doubtless accentuated by his lowly origin and limited education. Stalin's intellectual superiors—revolutionary colleagues and cloistered academicians alike—have been prone to minimize the intuitive skills of the born politician in belaboring the problem of how a drab mediocrity could have risen to a position of such lofty eminence.

Stalin's anomalous role as student and revolutionary propagandist ended in June 1899 when he was expelled from the school, ostensibly for failing to take his examinations. His later assertion that "propagating Marxism" was the real cause is plausible enough, for his teachers must have doubted his religious and political orthodoxy. But the reluctance of his official biographers to document the circumstances of his expulsion leaves the impression that the authorities had no knowledge of his outside activities. Whatever the technicalities concerning his departure, Stalin had long since broken with the suffocating ideology of the seminary, and it was with a profound sense of relief that he discarded this galling stigma of intellectual subservience. Yet his seminary training left an indelible imprint. He had learned Russian under religious auspices, and the flat, dogmatic style of his mature exposition, with its arid repetition, rhetorical questions, and theological metaphors were reminiscent of the litany and the catechism. He never mastered the grace and rhythm of the Russian language, and it remained a foreign tongue which he spoke with a Georgian accent to the end of his days.

For the balance of the year Stalin managed a precarious existence by private tutoring and by the generosity of seminary friends and fellow workers in the revolutionary movement. In January 1900 he obtained employment as a clerk in the Tiflis Geophysical Observatory. The pay was meager, but his duties were undemanding and left ample leisure to pursue his work with the *Mes-*

sameh Dassy. He made his first public speech at a May Day demonstration on the outskirts of the city. The vigilance of the secret police—the *Okhrana*—increased along with the pace of socialist agitation. In April 1901 the ringleaders were arrested, and the police raided Stalin's room at the observatory in his absence. Forced to abandon his job to avoid detection, he entered the clandestine life of a professional revolutionary. There was to be no turning back until the February Revolution in 1917 emptied the jails of political prisoners, released the administrative exiles from their Siberian bondage, and brought back the émigrés from Europe and America.

According to the Stalinist tradition, young Djugashvili soon became the leading revolutionary Marxist of the Transcaucasus. His actual accomplishments were more modest, though the arrest of his superiors in Tiflis made him by default one of the most prominent local activists. He helped organize an impressive May Day celebration in 1901, far more militant than the timid gathering of the previous year. Some two thousand workers clashed with police and Cossacks in the heart of the city, and of the demonstrators fourteen were wounded and over fifty arrested. *Iskra,* the chief organ of the Social Democratic party, hailed the news with delight: "This day marks the beginning of an open revolutionary movement in the Caucasus." [3]

Stalin fled to Gori, where he remained in hiding for several months. In November, having secretly returned to Tiflis, he was elected to the nine member committee of the local Social Democratic organization. In effect, the new body superseded the *Messameh Dassy* and temporarily became the ruling echelon of Transcaucasian socialism. Stalin left a few weeks later to establish party cells and spread revolutionary propaganda in Batum, an oil port on the Black Sea near the Turkish frontier. His precipitate departure seems to have been caused by a quarrel with his one time mentor, Sylvester Djibladze. The details are in dispute, but Menshevik sources charge Stalin with a campaign of slander and intrigue against his colleague leading to his expulsion from the Tiflis organization.

In Batum, Stalin assumed the underground party name Koba, a fictitious Georgian hero reminiscent of Robin Hood. If we can believe his official biographers, he was a veritable dynamo of revolutionary energy. He set up a secret printing press, wrote leaflets and supervised their distribution, organized strikes, and incited an unsuccessful attempt to storm the local jail to free three hundred striking workers. The police finally caught up with the elusive Koba on April 18, 1902, when he was imprisoned for the first of many times in his career.

Political offenders under the Tsarist regime enjoyed a higher status than ordinary criminals, and a revolutionary with a little money for extra privileges, an equable temperament, and some inner resources of the mind found the adjustment to prison life relatively easy. Koba was well endowed with patience and self-possession, so much so that to his fellow inmates he seemed unduly aloof. He spent much of his time reading, corresponded with party comrades on the outside, and took an active part in the discussions and debates allowed by the prison authorities. There was no trial and conviction for a specific crime: Koba was simply detained until the ponderous workings of the Tsarist bureaucracy could grind out a decision. In November 1903 he was finally exiled to eastern Siberia for a period of three years.

The Russian Social Democratic Labor party had meanwhile undergone a fateful split whose consequences even the most astute observer could not have foreseen. At a party congress held in Brussels and London during the previous summer—the Second Congress according to later Bolshevik nomenclature—the delegates had clashed over the outwardly simple issue of who should be admitted to the party and who should not. One faction, led by Vladimir Ilyich Lenin, insisted that members should form a highly disciplined elite willing to devote their lives to the revolutionary cause. The other, headed by Julius Martov, maintained that cooperation in furthering the aims of the party should be sufficient for membership. The controversy, of course, involved much more than the wording of a party statute, presumably the matter in dispute.

For several years there had been a growing cleavage among the leaders as to the aims and methods of the revolutionary struggle. In the inner circle—chiefly those who composed the editorial board of *Iskra*—these disagreements were recognized but concealed in the guise of temperamental rather than ideological differences. With something of a facetious air, they spoke among themselves of the "hards" and the "softs." Lenin, who reserved his fiercest invective for "revisionists" who would modify the sacred canons of Marxism, was clearly a "hard"; Martov, who looked to middle class liberalism as an ally, not an enemy, was obviously a "soft." Martov won his fight on the membership question, but Lenin managed to swing a scant majority to his side after a number of "soft" delegates had departed. Because of this technical and largely fortuitous "victory" the Leninists afterwards dubbed themselves the *bolshinstvo* (majority), while the Martovists passively accepted the label *menshinstvo* (minority). Unity between the factions proved impossible, and in time the Bolsheviks and Mensheviks formed two separate parties, each absorbed in vindicating its vision of the Marxist utopia on Russian soil.

In December 1903 Koba-Stalin arrived with a group of fellow deportees in the tiny village of Novaya Uda, some three hundred miles north of Irkutsk. The numbing cold of a Siberian winter would have deterred the average exile from any thought of escape until spring. Not so the tough and determined Koba. On January 18, little more than a month after his arrival, he slipped away from the settlement by sled and apparently made his way to Irkutsk. Traveling with a false passport, he was back in his old haunts in Tiflis by mid-February.

Koba's activities for the balance of the year are shrouded in obscurity. His official biographers are content with such unenlightening generalities as his supposed leadership of the Transcaucasian Bolsheviks: as "Lenin's faithful mainstay" in the Caucasus he conducted a "fierce fight against Menshevism." [4] He was, in reality, no more than an able underground worker with a local reputation. But there is no reason to doubt that when he had an opportunity to examine the issues involved in the party split he chose the Bolshevik faction. By temperament, environment, and training he represented the Leninist ideal of the "hard core" revolutionary whose Marxism was uncontaminated by the reformist tendencies of Western socialism or the sophisticated intellectualism of the Mensheviks.

During the summer Koba married Catherine (Keke) Svanidze, the sister of a former schoolmate at the Tiflis seminary. An attractive girl, she had received a conventional upbringing and did not share her husband's radical views. The ceremony apparently took place at an Orthodox church in Gori, obviously in deference to Keke's religious beliefs. The marriage, as far as we know, was a happy one. Koba made no attempt to apply Marxist principles of sex equality to his personal life, either then or later. The household was typically Georgian—male supremacy and female subservience. Keke's premature death in 1907 seems to have shaken the young revolutionary. A boyhood friend who attended the funeral recalls that Koba pointed to her coffin and said: "Soso, this creature softened my stony heart; she is dead and with her died my last warm feelings for humanity." [5]

The only offspring of the union, Yakov (Jacob), was raised by his maternal aunt in Tiflis and eventually studied in Moscow. As a young man his father treated him with cold contempt, and in the late twenties he attempted suicide while living in the Kremlin. He succeeded only in wounding himself, causing Stalin to remark scornfully: "Ha! He couldn't even shoot straight!" [6] Yakov became an electrical engineer and later graduated from Frunze Military Academy with the rank of lieutenant. He was captured near Smolensk in the early stages of World War II and perished in the Sachsenhausen concentration camp near Berlin in April 1943. The circumstances indicate virtual suicide, for he was shot while deliberately flouting camp regulations by touching the charged wire and calling out, "Guard, don't be cowardly!" [7] After the war Stalin offered a $250,000 reward in a German Communist newspaper for information as to his son's death but probably never learned the details.

In 1905 Russia was torn by strikes, mutinies, peasant revolt, and mass demonstrations. In retrospect, the abortive revolution of 1905 may be seen as the dress rehearsal for 1917. Neither the Bolsheviks nor Mensheviks distinguished themselves. Caught by surprise, they remained helpless bystanders as the nonparty St. Petersburg Soviet emerged as the leading organ of popular discontent. Only Leon Trotsky, of all the Social Democrats, achieved the stature of a revolutionary hero. In an attempt to rally his forces, Lenin called a Bolshevik conference at Tammerfors, Finland, in December 1905. Koba-Stalin attended as one of the Caucasian delegates and there met his chief for the first time. He was to recall the circumstances shortly after Lenin's death in 1924:

I was hoping to see the mountain eagle of our Party, the great man, great not only politically, but, if you will, physically, because in my imagination I had pictured Lenin as a giant, stately and imposing. What, then, was my disappointment to see a most ordinary-looking man, below average height, in no way, literally in no way, distinguishable from ordinary mortals. . . .

It is accepted as the usual thing for a "great man" to come late to meetings so that the assembly may await has appearance with baited breath; and then, just before the "great man" enters, the warning whisper goes up: "Hush! . . . Silence! . . . He's coming." This ritual did not seem to me superfluous, because it creates an impression, inspires respect. What, then, was my disappointment to learn Lenin had arrived . . . before the delegates, had settled himself somewhere in a corner, and was unassumingly carrying on a conversation, a most ordinary conversation with the most ordinary delegates. . . . I will not conceal from

you that at that time this seemed to me to be something of a violation
of certain essential rules.[8]

Stalin was offering a tribute to Lenin's modesty, but the passage is more significant as a self-portrait than as a contribution to
Leniniana. From the 1920's onward he seldom lost an opportunity to play the "great man" according to "certain essential
rules." Humility and self-effacement were never among his virtues, though when it suited his purpose he could dissemble his
vanity with the facility of a professional actor.

The revolutionary wave had already receded by the time of the
Tammerfors conference. Unwilling to admit that the Tsarist regime had regained at least a temporary measure of stability, the
Social Democrats sought to reconcile their differences in preparation for the struggle that lay ahead. A "unity congress" met at
Stockholm in the spring of 1906, and for six years the Bolsheviks
and Mensheviks strove to achieve a semblance of party unity.
Koba-Stalin, then using the name Ivanovich, was the only Bolshevik among the eleven delegates from the Caucasus. It was his first
journey abroad. As in his other trips outside Russia—all of them
on party business—he had neither the time nor the inclination to
sample the cosmopolitan charms of western Europe. His insular-
ity, unleavened by intellectual curiosity or the internationalism
of the socialist creed, would in time become a major asset as
Bolshevism and Russian nationalism merged in Stalinism.

Koba played no role of consequence in the Stockholm Congress.
Only his subsequent fame led to a diligent search of party annals
for indications of his presence. The Bolsheviks, outnumbered and
outvoted, were dismayed. Lenin, according to Stalin's later account, faced adversity with courage and resolution:

I remember that we, the Bolshevik delegates, huddled together in a
group, gazing at Lenin and asking his advice. The speeches of some of
the delegates betrayed a note of weariness and dejection. I recall that
to these speeches Lenin bitingly replied through clenched teeth: "Don't
whine, comrades, we are bound to win, for we are right." Hatred of
the whining intellectual, faith in our own strength, confidence in victory—that is what Lenin impressed upon us.[9]

A year later, when another congress met in London, party for-
tunes were still at a low ebb, though the Bolsheviks had a slight
majority. Koba attended (again as Ivanovich), this time in a
"consultative" capacity, for he had been unable to obtain voting

credentials from the weak Causasian Bolshevik movement. There he saw his future rival, Trotsky, for the first time. He shared the rather contemptuous attitude of the Bolsheviks toward the young firebrand of 1905, then attempting to organize his own faction. Reporting on the congress in a clandestine Bolshevik newspaper published in Baku, Koba-Ivanovich (as he signed himself) referred to Trotsky as "pretty but useless," apparently quoting a remark that Lenin had already made. In an analysis of the ethnic composition of the congress, he pointed out that a majority of the Menshevik delegates were Jews. "In this connection," he wrote, "one of the Bolsheviks (I think it was Comrade Alexinsky) observed in jest that the Mensheviks constituted a Jewish group while the Bolsheviks constituted a true-Russian group, and, therefore, it wouldn't be a bad idea for us Bolsheviks to organize a pogrom in the Party." [10] The passage might be dismissed as a harmless joke were it not for the pronounced anti-Semitism that Stalin was to reveal in later life.

On June 25, 1907, a spectacular armed robbery of state funds in Tiflis once again focused the party's attention upon the question of revolutionary "expropriations." Banditry to replenish the party coffers—a practice that flourished among the "fighting squads" of the Caucasus—had been condemned at the Stockholm and London congresses, but Lenin was never overly scrupulous about the source of his funds and winked at this "apache deviation." He maintained contact with these Bolshevik freebooters through Koba, whose services were so discreet that even now it is impossible to determine his precise role in the expropriations. The Tiflis robbery was led by Semyon Ter-Petrosyan, a brave and audacious Armenian known to his associates as Kamo. He and Koba were boyhood friends, and the legend has persisted despite the paucity of evidence that Kamo acted as Koba's disciple in carrying out the Tiflis raid and other sensational exploits in the Caucasus. Stalin himself preserved an unbroken silence on this aspect of his career. Only his unofficial and more romantic biographers have sought to cast an aura of derring-do over his Caucasian adventures. The Mensheviks were scandalized by the Tiflis affair and Lenin's ill-concealed contempt for the party mandate. The Bolsheviks gained little if any financial advantage from the coup, for the stolen rubles—estimated at 341,000 or $170,500 at the official rate of exchange—were almost all in 500 ruble notes and could not be exchanged in either Russian or foreign banks without arousing suspicion.

During the summer of 1907 Koba settled in Baku. The local oil workers furnished the sole example of proletarian militancy in a country that to all appearances had succumbed to the torpor of political reaction. "Three [two?] years of revolutionary activity among the workers in the oil industry," Stalin recalled in 1926, "steeled me as a practical fighter and as one of the local practical leaders. Association with . . . advanced workers in Baku . . . and the storm of acute conflicts between the workers and the oil owners . . . first taught me what it means to lead large masses of workers. . . . I thus received my second baptism in the revolutionary struggle. There I became a journeyman in the art of revolution." [11] He had indeed passed beyond the apprentice level, but no one, least of all the astute Lenin, considered the young Georgian of sufficient intellectual stature to be counted among the leaders of Bolshevism. He was valued for what he was—an efficient "practical" whose contribution to the cause could best be made in the front lines of the revolution. Although he would no doubt have been flattered by a summons to western Europe, he was proud of his underground status and looked upon the exiles —always excepting Lenin—with a mixture of envy and disdain as an effete group unable to endure the hardships of day-to-day revolutionary activity.

Like the other expendables of the Bolshevik cadre, Koba could not expect to outwit the police indefinitely. In April 1908 he was arrested for the second time and lodged in the local prison, a crowded and more stringent institution than the jail in Batum. A fellow inmate, a Socialist Revolutionary, was impressed by Koba's cool nerves, his "rudeness in controversy," and his "mechanical memory" of the Marxist classics. The following November Koba was deported to the province of Vologda in the northern part of European Russia. His relatively lenient sentence of two years indicates that the *Okhrana* had been unable to link him with specific acts of an illegal nature. In March 1909, after a layover on the journey caused by a bout with typhus, he reached his place of banishment, the town of Solvychegodsk. In July he contrived to escape—there was only nominal surveillance for exiles in his category. He stayed for several days with a Bolshevik sympathizer in St. Petersburg, contacted party headquarters, and received an unofficial assignment as the Caucasian correspondent for the Social Democratic press abroad.

Traveling with a false passport under still another alias, Koba returned to Baku late in July. The party organization had languished during his absence, and labor conditions in the oil fields had worsened despite a boom in production. The local party organ, *Bakinsky Proletary,* had ceased publication, and Koba managed to revive it shortly after his return. His methods of fund raising were unorthodox—indeed unsavory—if the allegation contained in one of his biographies is correct. According to this undocumented account, he levied special assessments on shopkeepers and other businessmen. If they refused to pay or complained to the police, his henchmen, who included professional criminals, beat up the victims or wrecked their property. He is also said to have organized a chain of brothels in various Caucasian towns, and when Lenin warned of a possible scandal he obligingly sacrificed his proprietary interests in favor of a "protection service" for street prostitutes.[12]

There is nothing inherently improbable about this supposed racketeering interlude in Stalin's career, for he would scarcely have found his duties morally repugnant. The sacred cause of the revolution furnished ample justification for the deeds done in its name. But the vast accretion of rumor, gossip, legend, and fabrication about the great Kremlin despot makes proper authentication even more imperative. Better publicized—and equally devoid of supporting data—is the charge that Stalin was an informer for the *Okhrana* during these years. Its credibility rests upon a flimsy compound of conjecture and circumstantial evidence, bolstered by a document that purports to be the letter of a Tsarist police official written in 1913. Unfortunately for the proponents of the "agent" hypothesis, the letter bears all the earmarks of a none too skillful forgery.[13]

Koba-Stalin was nothing if not versatile. He aspired to a certain intellectual standing, and for the first time succeeded in publishing an article in a journal of more than provincial circulation. The first of his two "Letters From the Caucasus"—factual, meaty, and without literary embellishment—appeared in *Sotsial Demokrat,* the émigré organ of the combined party. In March 1910, less than a month later, Koba was arrested and confined once more to the prison in Baku. In September he was ordered to complete his two year term of exile at Solvychegodsk. Obviously the authorities did not yet consider him a formidable threat to the established order.

CHAPTER III

Exile, Revolution, and Civil War

FROM THE TIME OF HIS THIRD ARREST IN 1910 TO THE COLLAPSE OF the Tsarist regime in 1917 Koba-Stalin spent less than a year as a free man—that is, in the precarious freedom permitted to an active revolutionary. For more than six years he was either in prison or in administrative exile. Yet this is the period when the traditional refrain of anti-Stalinist folklore—that of the mediocre and anonymous party hack—clashes head-on with Stalinist hagiography, in which Koba is no longer merely the leading Bolshevik of the Caucasus but Lenin's most trusted and faithful disciple. Neither interpretation is warranted.

Although Koba's limitations as a theorist were obvious, Lenin valued him for precisely those qualities of loyalty, discipline, perseverance, and political astuteness that he sometimes despaired of finding among his quarrelsome and precocious colleagues. Accordingly, in January 1912 he proposed Koba as a member of the Bolshevik Central Committee when a small group of Social Democrats, chiefly of the Leninist persuasion, gathered in Prague to signal their formal break with the Mensheviks. As Lenin saw it, the farce of party unity could no longer be maintained without sacrifice of revolutionary principle. His Georgian protegé failed of election, but he later insisted that the Central Committee exercise its right to co-opt additional members. Koba therefore joined a Bolshevik elite of nine, of whom the most outstanding (in terms of later notoriety) were of course Lenin himself, whose supremacy over the party was unquestioned despite its unofficial character; Gregory Zinoviev, an intellectual of Jewish origin and one of Lenin's oldest and closest collaborators; Gregory (Sergo) Ordjonikidze, a Georgian comrade of Koba's; and Roman Malinovsky, a Russified Pole and secret police agent who was to be shot by the Soviet government in 1918 when his dual career had been disclosed.

Koba, meanwhile, had completed his term of exile at Solvychegodsk in July 1911. Forbidden to return to the Caucasus or to reside in any of Russia's leading metropolitan centers, he was al-

lowed to settle in Vologda, a provincial city strategically placed
east of St. Petersburg and north of Moscow. In September he visited the capital illegally but was picked up within two days. After
three months' detention, he was deported to Vologda for three
years—again a comparatively mild sentence. He received the
news of his promotion to the Central Committee from Ordjonikidze, who visited him late in February of 1912. Soon afterward
Koba eluded the cursory police surveillance in Vologda and returned to the Caucasus for conferences with party workers in
Tiflis and Baku. On April 23 he arrived in St. Petersburg and as
the highest ranking Bolshevik took over the editorship of *Zvezda*
("The Star"), the party weekly. Also, according to the official
chronology, he helped found *Pravda* as a daily newspaper, the
inaugural issue of which appeared on May 5, the same day the
police picked him up once more. This time Koba was deemed
important enough to be sent to a remote village in western Siberia. But in September, about six weeks after reaching his new
place of detention, he contrived his fourth escape.

Koba reappeared in St. Petersburg in time to participate in the
election campaign for deputies to the fourth Duma, the national
assembly established by imperial decree during the revolution of
1905. The Bolsheviks won six seats, the Mensheviks seven. The
electoral commission attempted to invalidate the result in several
Petersburg factories—so radical were the electors chosen by the
workers—but withdrew its ruling in the face of a strike initiated
"by the representative of the Central Committee." [1] Thus Koba,
with outward modesty, reported his part in the election campaign
to *Sotsial Demokrat*. For the first time he used the pseudonym "K.
Stalin" in a signed contribution. Henceforth the Koba of his
Georgian past was replaced by the more appropriate revolutionary alias of Stalin ("Man of Steel").

In November, Stalin made his way to Cracow, a Polish city
then under Austrian rule, for a brief meeting with Lenin. The
Bolshevik chieftain was dissatisfied by the conciliationist tactics of
the party's Duma representatives and demanded a complete divorce from the Mensheviks. Stalin, who was in a better position to
gauge the sentiment among the rank and file, gave only lip service to what seemed to him an impolitic move. Early in 1913 he
again journeyed to Cracow at Lenin's invitation for a conference
with members of the Central Committee and the party's Duma
representation. Lenin had misgivings about Stalin's political
judgment, but he tactfully concealed them by detaining him for
various assignments, chiefly literary. Jacob Sverdlov, the future

president of the Soviet Union, was dispatched to the Russian capital as a more pliable instrument of Lenin's will.

Stalin remained in Cracow—with a side trip to Vienna—for approximately six weeks. A shrewd judge of men, Lenin had an extended opportunity to examine the personal qualities and mental resources of his Georgian disciple. He was not displeased, and in certain areas—notably Stalin's grasp of Caucasian affairs —he was impressed. Their talks touched on the intricacies of the nationality question in the Caucasus, and Lenin proposed that he explore the topic of nationalism on a broader scale as a possible contribution to the party's theoretical journal. Under Lenin's general supervision Stalin worked energetically at the task and produced a lengthy essay of modest distinction, subsequently known as "Marxism and the National Question." Lenin was delighted and wrote to the novelist Maxim Gorky: "We have a wonderful Georgian here who has sat down to write a big article for *Prosveshchenie* ["Enlightenment"] after collecting *all* the Austrian and other material." [2] For the first time the Bolshevik viewpoint on the nationality problem, especially as it applied to the Russian empire, was presented in a systematic fashion. Lenin's notion that cultural self-determination was insufficient—that separation might include political autonomy or even national independence—was explored within the framework of Marxist theory. But Stalin was more cautious than the Bolshevik program on nationalities that Lenin was to formulate: he advocated only regional autonomy for minorities along cultural lines. Although less ephemeral than polemical journalism, the essay would have remained in the limbo of socialist exegesis but for the author's later renown. Lacking a comparable example of literary prowess, Stalin's sycophants were to embalm it as a Marxist classic. Stalin derived a good deal of personal satisfaction from his performance, for now he too could be counted among the ideologues of the party; and his reputation was established as the leading Bolshevik authority on the problem of nationalities.

In late February of 1913 Stalin returned to St. Petersburg. Only a few days before, Sverdlov, Lenin's emissary, had been arrested, and within a week Stalin himself was taken into custody. Ironically, he was a victim of his colleague, the *Okhrana* agent Malinovsky, who had been elected as a Bolshevik representative to the Duma from Moscow. The police, informed beforehand, arrested him at a fund-raising concert sponsored by the local party organization. Too important a captive for routine treatment, he was exiled for four years to the Turukhansk district of northern Siberia near the Arctic Circle. In this desolate region, hundreds of miles from the nearest railroad or metropolis, the opportunities for escape were few. In August, Stalin reached his final destination, the tiny settlement of Kostino, where Sverdlov had preceded him.

Lenin hoped that the two exiles could manage to escape and sent them money for expenses. But he made the mistake of confiding in Malinovsky, who promptly informed the authorities. Precautions were redoubled, and in March 1914 Stalin and Sverdlov were transferred farther north to Kureika on the Yenisei River. The two men shared a room, an arrangement that Sverdlov found overly confining. "He [Stalin] is a good chap," he wrote to his sister, "but too much of an individualist in everyday life, while I believe in at least a semblance of order." Their estrangement grew, and Sverdlov complained in another letter of "a number of encounters (personal conflicts), possible only in the conditions of prison and exile, their pettiness notwithstanding, [which] have had a pretty strong effect on my nerves." [3] He later secured a transfer to another village.

The solitude and monotony of a life in exile can undermine even the most cheerful personality, and from all accounts Stalin found it difficult to sustain a warm personal relationship under the best of circumstances. In the wilderness of Turukhansk he seemed to retreat within himself, seldom making the effort to contact other political exiles in the area. He led an active outdoor life—hunting, fishing, and trapping—and read a good deal. But for some unexplained reason he did little writing. His only serious effort, another article on the nationalities question, was never published. Very likely Lenin considered it inferior work. The editors of Stalin's collected writings and speeches, in attempting to conceal an embarrassing hiatus of nearly four years in his literary production, make the dubious claim that the nationalities piece "and a number of other works, have not yet been discovered."

With the outbreak of war in 1914 the prospect of escape—never very encouraging—seemed hopeless. To live illegally in wartime Russia was a precarious undertaking even if Stalin somehow could have reached a major urban center. Like most of the exiles, he decided to wait for peace or the expiration of his term. At times his sense of loneliness must have been overwhelming. In a letter to his future mother-in-law, Olga Alliluyeva, he gave a rare glimpse of his personal feelings. Thanking her for a food parcel, he urged her not to spend any more money because she was in greater need than he. "I shall be satisfied if from time to time you send me a postcard with a view of nature and so forth. In this accursed country nature is reduced to barren ugliness—in summer the river, in winter the snow—and that's all the nature there is. I am stupidly homesick for the sight of a landscape, if only on paper." [4]

In March 1917 the dull tedium of the long Siberian winter was interrupted by sensational news from the capital. The Tsar had fallen, and with him the whole edifice of political autocracy had collapsed with a suddenness that startled veterans of the revolutionary struggle. War exhaustion had accomplished what decades of propaganda and agitation had failed to do. The heroes of the revolution were the anonymous citizens and soldiers of Petrograd. (The city had been renamed for patriotic reasons in 1914.) They were not consulted by the middle class liberals of the Duma, who proceeded to establish a democratic Provisional Government devoted to the successful prosecution of the war and the indefinite postponement of domestic problems. The masses had more confidence in the Soviet of Workers' Deputies, a newly revived organ of revolutionary democracy that had succumbed to Tsarist repression in 1905. But the Soviet, then composed of moderate socialists, refused to take power and thereby created a vacuum in political authority that the "legal" Provisional Government strove in vain to fill.

Stalin had been allowed to serve the last months of his sentence in Achinsk, a sizable town located on the main line of the Trans-Siberian Railway. A fellow exile there has left a lively if unflattering appraisal of Stalin:

[He] usually remained taciturn and morose, placidly smoking his pipe filled with atrocious *makhorka* [cheap tobacco]. . . . His education was very deficient and . . . the main stock of his ideas was borrowed from popular . . . Socialist pamphlets. It was equally plain to me that he was a narrow-minded, fanatical man. . . . Neither was there any personal charm about him which sometimes gives a man a kind of magnetic power. His appearance was rather repellant; his manners were coarse; his general attitude towards other people was rude, provocative, and cynical.[5]

These observations tally closely with what we know from other sources, though hindsight and the possibility of personal or political bias cannot be dismissed.

The political amnesty allowed Stalin to leave for Petrograd on

March 21 with a number of other exiles, of whom Leo Kamenev was the most prominent. Their arrival four days later went virtually unnoticed as a political event, but in Bolshevik circles the appearance of the second rank leadership—Lenin and his chief lieutenants were still abroad—was a momentous occasion. As the senior member of the Central Committee in the capital, Stalin felt that he was entitled to take over the local party organization and the editorship of *Pravda*. But his abrasive personality had not endeared him to the lesser Bolsheviks, and the self-constituted Russian Bureau of the Central Committee "expressed itself in favor of asking him to attend in a consultative capacity" because of "certain personal traits." [6] This stinging blow to his pride so offended Stalin that he proceeded to conduct a purge of the *Pravda* staff on his own authority. The Bolshevik organ had been edited by an inexperienced young trio, including the future Soviet foreign minister Vyacheslav Molotov. They had pursued a "Leftist" course—that is, critical of the Provisional Government and its war policy, while other Bolsheviks called for collaboration with the Mensheviks and a defense of the Revolution against German imperialism. Stalin, with Kamenev and Matvei Muranov as co-editors, backed away from the militance of his predecessors, striving for the role of compromiser. "The stark slogan, 'Down with the war!' is absolutely unsuitable" as a practical means of ending the struggle, he wrote in *Pravda*. "The solution is to bring pressure on the Provisional Government to make it . . . start peace negotiations immediately." [7] From the standpoint of Leninist orthodoxy it was a grave doctrinal error, for it implied passive support of a bourgeois government. But in Lenin's absence the Bolsheviks on the scene were bewildered and disoriented by a revolutionary situation that had not been foreseen in the Marxist handbooks.

Lenin had been frantically seeking a way back to Russia from Switzerland. At length, through negotiations with the German government, he obtained passage on the so-called "sealed train" across Germany and arrived in Petrograd via Sweden and Finland on April 16. He lost no time in pulling his followers up short by assailing the conciliationism of *Pravda* and launching a full scale verbal offensive against the Provisional Government. Even the radicals in the party were stunned. Nikolai Sukhanov, a nonparty socialist, recalls the occasion: "I shall never forget that thunder-like speech, which startled and amazed not only me, a heretic who accidentally dropped in, but all the true believers." Lenin wisely avoided the wounding phrases of personal recrimination and gave his disciples time to adjust to his sweeping pronunciamento. A few, such as Kamenev, continued to harbor doubts, and a small Right wing group left the fold altogether. Stalin was one of the first to embrace the new dispensation, conceding later that he had shared a mistaken position with the majority of the party. He retained the editorship of *Pravda,* and on May 11 he was elected to the new Central Committee at a conference representing about 76,000 members.

Although by any objective standard Stalin played a major if not significant part in the events leading to the Bolshevik Revolution, his detractors have consistently attempted to minimize his importance and to demean his talents. The Stalinists, on the other hand, have inflated their hero beyond recognition and libeled his political opponents to the point of caricature.

Trotsky, who was to inspire much of the anti-Stalinist depreciation on the faulty premise that the Georgian revolutionary was a nonentity prior to the mid-twenties, did not himself join the party until July 1917. As a latecomer and a Marxist of international reputation, he was bound to arouse resentment among the Old Bolsheviks. One may conjecture that Stalin was jealous of this brilliant parvenu, yet it would be misleading to make their future antagonism retroactive. The two had met briefly in Vienna in 1913, and Trotsky later claimed that he could recall a "glint of animosity" in Stalin's "yellow eyes." Shortly before their meeting Stalin had described him in *Sotsial Demokrat* as a "noisy champion with fake muscles," but the gibe was only the common coin of sectarian politics and mild compared to the taunts that Lenin and Trotsky had exchanged. Writing in 1929, Trotsky depicted Stalin as a political cipher during the Revolution: "He never made any public appearance to defend Lenin's views; he merely stood back and waited. During the most responsible months of the theoretical and political preparation for the [Bolshevik] uprising, Stalin simply did not exist in the political sense." [8] Sukhanov was even less flattering. Stalin, he wrote, "produced . . . the impression of a grey blur, looming up now and then dimly and not leaving any trace. There is really nothing more to be said about him." [9]

There was, of course, much more to Stalin's role in 1917 than that of the faceless functionary, obediently performing the petty chores delegated by his political superiors. True, he lacked the eloquence of the effective stump orator and the polished style of the practiced journalist. He stayed behind the scenes, unknown to the public but a respected veteran to the party vanguard despite his lack of personal popularity. Aside from his editorial duties, he was the principal intermediary between the Central Committee and the Bolshevik cadres in the factories, the regiments, and the Petrograd Soviet.

Lenin was content to allow the Revolution to ripen without forcing the pace by armed demonstrations or appeals for insurrection. The chief Bolshevik slogan, "All Power to the Soviets!," was a demand that the moderate socialists accept the responsibility that the Provisional Government increasingly demonstrated its incapacity to meet. The radical temper of the workers and soldiers outran the prudent calculations of the Bolsheviks. In mid-July anarchy reigned in the streets as some 20,000 sailors from the nearby naval base at Kronstadt joined the angry protest against the government and its pusillanimous ally, the Soviet Executive Committee. A determined band of armed men could have taken power with ease, but whether they could have held it for more than a few days is debatable. Lenin and his cohorts wrestled with the delicate task of curbing their overly enthusiastic followers without betraying the party's militant image. The leaderless and frustrated demonstrators finally dispersed, and the episode known as the July Days ended as spontaneously as it had begun. The government ministers, regaining their courage with the appearance of loyal troops, blamed the Bolsheviks for the disorders. Soldiers seized party headquarters, and *Pravda* was proscribed after its offices and printing press were wrecked. Stalin helped to avoid bloodshed by negotiating the surrender of the rebel-held Peter and Paul Fortress.

The Bolsheviks were not formally outlawed, but until September they operated on a semi-clandestine basis. The Ministry of Justice released some dubious evidence that Lenin and his colleagues were German agents, a charge that was taken up by the Right wing press and gained wide currency in popular opinion. Lenin and Zinoviev were indicted, and to avoid arrest and possible murder while in custody they went into hiding. Trotsky, Kamenev, and a number of lesser figures were imprisoned; Stalin, who had attracted little attention, was the highest ranking Bolshevik still at large. Lenin stayed a few days in the apartment of Stalin's friend and future father-in-law, Sergei Alliluyev, and eventually found a safe haven in Finland, still a semi-autonomous part of the Russian empire.

The surface impression that the Bolsheviks had been crushed—or at the very least had suffered a sharp setback—overlooked their growing strength in Petrograd, Moscow, and other industrial cities. In August, when the Sixth Congress was held, the party membership (about 240,000) had more than tripled in three months. The Bolshevik cadre was intact, and the temporary loss of the top echelon was more an inconvenience than a disability. Lenin's instructions to the Central Committee were delivered by messenger to the Alliluyev apartment, where Stalin resided. The Provisional Government, reorganized to include Mensheviks and Socialist Revolutionaries from the Petrograd Soviet, showed no greater disposition to bring the war to an end or to settle the land question to the satisfaction of the peasants.

Russia's conservatives, to whom the various brands of socialism were equally obnoxious, despaired of restoring order and discipline under the feeble leadership of the Provisional Government and its vacillating premier, Alexander Kerensky. They turned hopefully to the idea of dictatorship, and as a prime candidate for the strong man role they began to look with favor upon General Lavr Kornilov, the army's newly appointed commander-in-chief. The Bolshevik press had long been alert to a "counter-revolutionary conspiracy against the workers," to use the routine phrase of Stalin's editorial of August 21 in *Rabochy i Soldat* ("Worker and Soldier"), *Pravda's* interim replacement. With Kornilov's appearance as a distinct threat to the whole spectrum of the Center and Left, Stalin and his associates had a tangible apparition to exorcise. On September 8, under the guise of suppressing a Bolshevik plot, the general ordered his troops to march on Petrograd. Panic stricken, the government appealed for assistance—agitators to sap the morale of the attackers and Red Guards to defend the city. The Bolsheviks joined a "popular front" with the Mensheviks and Socialist Revolutionaries, political tactics that would be revived in the struggle against fascism two decades later.

The Kornilovite conspiracy collapsed without a shot being fired—the general's troops simply melted away as the monarchy and its supporters had disintegrated during the February Revolution. The Bolshevik seizure of power, which occurred less than two months later, was a direct legacy of the Kornilov fiasco. To the workers and soldiers the "bourgeoisie" were now thoroughly discredited, and the trend to Bolshevism gained enormous impetus. On September 13, as a result of by-elections, the Petrograd Soviet returned a Bolshevik majority, and five days later the Moscow Soviet followed the example of the capital. Trotsky and his fellow prisoners had been released on bail, but Lenin remained in Finland.

Late in September Lenin became convinced that the revolutionary crisis had matured and demanded that the Central Committee begin preparations for an immediate insurrection. "History will not forgive us," he remonstrated, "if we do not assume power now." Again, as in April, he constituted a minority of one. In its first crude formulation the scheme seemed sheer adventurism to his colleagues, but Lenin's iron will and powers of persuasion worked the customary transformation in the Central Committee. Only Zinoviev and Kamenev held out against their chief and flouted party discipline by attacking the decision in a non-Bolshevik newspaper. Lenin angrily called for the ouster of the two "strikebreakers," and Stalin took it upon himself to soften the statement by adding an editorial note in the party organ: "The sharp tone of Lenin's article does not alter the fact that in fundamentals we remain of one opinion." This mild rebuke of Lenin was scarcely accurate—what could have been more fundamental than a disagreement over revolutionary strategy? It subjected Stalin to the criticism of the Central Committee, though apparently he was seeking to heal the party rift, not to open a path for retreat in case the uprising failed (as Trotsky later charged). When Kamenev offered to resign from the Committee, Stalin voted with the minority in favor of retaining him. He then submitted his resignation from the board of editors. Unlike Kamenev's, it was not accepted.

By early November the Bolsheviks hardly bothered to conceal their preparations for a coup d'état. Party headquarters had been reestablished at Smolny Institute, once a fashionable finishing school for young ladies. The Military Revolutionary Committee, the general staff of the insurgents, planned the details of the campaign under Trotsky's supervision. In the early morning hours of November 7 the Red Guard, the workers' militia organized prior to the Kornilov revolt, occupied the strategic buildings of Petrograd. With the fall of the Winter Palace—the site of the Provisional Government—late that evening the Bolshevik Revolution was accomplished with almost ridiculous ease. Less than a dozen casualties marked the greatest revolutionary upheaval of the twentieth century. The bloodletting was to come later—three agonizing years of civil war and foreign intervention.

Throughout the stirring events of the "great October Socialist Revolution," long since enshrined in party history and legend, one name is unaccountably missing—that of Stalin. He was absent from the Central Committee meeting on November 6 that launched the insurrection and did not make an appearance at

Smolny later that day. The classic eyewitness account of the Bolshevik rising, *Ten Days That Shook the World* by the radical American journalist John Reed, virtually ignores him. (This was sufficient reason to ban it during the Stalin era.) Trotsky has maliciously suggested that he was deliberately absent: "The cautious schemer preferred to stay on the fence at the crucial moment. He was waiting to see how the insurrection turned out before committing himself to a position." [10] This interpretation is flatly contradicted by his previous votes in the Central Committee and by his editorials—usually unsigned—in the party organ. These were not the actions of a "cautious schemer" trying to cover his tracks. Presumably Stalin was attending to his editorial duties during these critical hours, but his remoteness from the centers of political action was discomfiting to his official biographers and court historians. In order to create a more heroic image, they fashioned a new post for Stalin at the head of the "party center" which allegedly directed the seizure of power. Such an organ was created on paper in October, but there is no evidence that it ever functioned. His biographical chronicle for 1917 is succinct and slightly less outrageous in its claim: "V. I. Lenin and J. V. Stalin direct the October armed uprising."

In 1918, marking the anniversary of the October days, Stalin paid a generous and unequivocal tribute to Trotsky in the party press: "All the work of practical organization of the insurrection was conducted under the direct leadership of the President of the Petrograd Soviet, Comrade Trotsky. It may be said with certainty that the swift passing of the garrison to the side of the Soviet, and the bold execution of the work of the Military Revolutionary Committee, the Party owes principally and above all to Comrade Trotsky." But revisionism proceeded swiftly, and within ten years his name was seldom mentioned in connection with the events of 1917. By the mid-thirties Stalin's scribes condemned him retroactively as a counter-revolutionary, and the official version of the Bolshevik Revolution reviled him as a "braggart and traitor" who had adopted a "Menshevik position" in secretly trying to sabotage the insurrection.[11]

On November 8 the Second Congress of Soviets approved the new Bolshevik government. The executive organ, the Council of People's Commissars, included Lenin as chairman and Trotsky as commissar for foreign affairs. As the party's expert on nationalities, Stalin was given the cabinet portfolio dealing with the subject —a position that neither the Tsarist regime nor the Provisional

Government had deemed important enough to create. If the governmental hierarchy had been constructed along the traditional lines of a parliamentary democracy, he would have been a relatively minor figure in affairs of state. But as one of the elder statesmen of the party's Central Committee he was now among the half-dozen most powerful men in Russia. Nevertheless, the political glamour of Lenin and Trotsky so far overshadowed him that he was in no sense a leader of national reputation.

The Commissariat of Nationality Affairs began in humble circumstances with a single "dark and malodorous" room in Smolny Institute. His secretary was Nadezhda Alliluyeva, the attractive daughter of his old comrade. In March 1918, when the government moved to Moscow, Stalin and his bureau heads acquired offices in the Kremlin and in various private homes expropriated from wealthy citizens of the old regime. His chief assistant has written a droll account of how Stalin, equipped with paper signs and thumb tacks, attempted to commandeer a hotel occupied by another commissariat. The two arrived after office hours, found a back entrance, and since the lights were not working, used matches to prowl the hallways, fastening notices on a number of doors at random to announce the new tenants. When their matches ran out they groped around in pitch darkness and ended up in the basement, where Stalin stumbled and fell, "nearly breaking his neck." [12] These nocturnal labors were in vain, however, for the Commissariat of Nationalities never did acquire the prized hotel.

The revolutionary romanticism with which the Bolsheviks took up the reins of power was soon eroded by the harsh realities of political life. One of the first illusions to expire was Lenin's notion that the national minorities should be free to secede from the Russian empire. Stalin gallantly tried to implement this item in the Leninist canon, and his first significant act as commissar for nationalities was to convey fraternal greetings to the Finnish Social Democratic party in Helsinki and to promise "complete freedom for the Finnish people." Little more than a month later—on December 31, 1917—Lenin and Stalin signed the formal decree granting independence. However low the fires of idealism were eventually to burn in Soviet Russia, Stalin always stood by the original decision on Finland when he might easily have annexed this small neighbor.

By the beginning of 1918, when anti-Bolshevik separatist movements had already appeared in the Ukraine, the Baltic region, the Caucasus, Central Asia, and Siberia, the party was forced to reexamine the fallacious logic of self-determination. No state, even one based on utopian socialist principles, could expect to endure as a functioning sovereignty with its borderlands an ethnic checkerboard of "independent" nations. Stalin proclaimed the new rationale at a session of the Congress of Soviets in January: self-determination should be the right of the laboring masses, not the bourgeoisie, "and should be subordinated to the principles of socialism." The constitutional façade was erected in July after a drafting commission, in which Stalin took a prominent role, submitted a proposal outlining the federal basis of the Soviet Republic. The Congress of Soviets, theoretically the supreme legislative body, had its counterpart at the regional, provincial, county, and district level. The party, where political power continued to reside, was not mentioned. Something of a stopgap measure, the 1918 constitution was replaced in July 1923 by a new document formally establishing the Union of Soviet Socialist Republics. The new constitution was more clearly Stalin's creation, and its genuflection toward the principle of national self-determination expressed his notion of the monolithic party camouflaged by a dazzling array of "democratic" and "autonomous" institutions.

Stalin's cabinet duties took up only part of his time. They were to a large extent ceremonial—receiving delegations and making speeches—and his other activities involved a wide range of administrative duties delegated by Lenin. If the Bolshevik chief had not fully appreciated Stalin's capabilities before the October Revolution, he now had ample opportunity to test them under a variety of circumstances. He found, too, that seasoned party members upon whom he could rely without question were in short supply. Zinoviev and Kamenev had wavered during the crisis of the October days, though they were outwardly restored to the good graces of the party; Trotsky, brilliant but vain and temperamental, deserted Lenin at a crucial moment during the intraparty struggle over the peace negotiations at Brest-Litovsk; Nikolai Bukharin, a promising young theoretician, joined the so-called Left Communist faction in advocating a "revolutionary war" against Germany; Sverdlov, one of the few consistent "Leninists," died of a lung infection in March 1919. Almost by default, therefore, Lenin came to rely on Stalin for the stolid virtues of a "good Bolshevik"—toughness, resolution, practicality, and a seeming immunity to the disease of "infantile Leftism" that threatened to wreck the party.

. . .

When the Treaty of Brest-Litovsk finally brought the war with Germany to an official close in March 1918, the outlying portions of the Russian empire had already broken away. Armed opposition to the Bolshevik regime was still feeble and uncoordinated, but the embryonic White armies were soon to receive moral and material support from the Allied powers. Stalin's first important assignment in the developing civil war was a mission to Tsaritsyn, the Volga city that was to become famous during World War II as Stalingrad. Charged with relieving the food shortage and arranging for grain shipments to Moscow and other industrial centers, he arrived on June 6 with an armed escort of several hundred men and two armored trains. "Chaos and profiteering" were rife, he reported to Lenin by telegram. He introduced rationing and price controls, untangled the snarl in rail transport, and arrested the chief trade agent for speculation in government goods. He also established a local branch of the Cheka—the secret police— to stamp out counter-revolutionary activity. The deteriorating military situation prevented his intended journey to the Caucasus, and on July 7 he asked Lenin for emergency authority to help salvage the front and restore the rail network south of Tsaritsyn. Three days later he complained bitterly to Lenin that Trotsky, now commissar for war, had appointed commanders in the south "without the knowledge of the local people"—meaning, presumably, that Stalin himself had not been consulted. Having failed to receive a reply to his previous request for special military powers, he declared that he would "dismiss army commanders and commissars who are ruining the work. . . . Not having a paper from Trotsky is not going to deter me." [13]

This was the opening salvo in the notorious quarrel between Trotsky and the "Tsaritsyn group." The latter included the ranking officers of the Tenth Red Army: Ordjonikidze, Stalin's old Georgian crony, the political commissar; Kliment Voroshilov, a former party colleague from Baku, the military commander; and Semyon Budyonny, a cavalry officer who had already acquired a reputation for guerrilla tactics. Stalin's sponsorship of the Tsaritsyn group, while it may have rested in part on questions of military strategy, was basically political. The amenities required by his party position barely concealed his resentment of Trotsky. The arrogant upstart of only a year ago had become the world famous leader of the Bolshevik Revolution and the commander of the Red Army. Stalin, on the other hand, still labored in obscurity, consumed by pride, envy, and a fierce determination to surpass his rival in the mechanics of power if not in public esteem.

Trotsky eventually found it necessary to seek Lenin's intervention. There could be no question of Trotsky's ultimate authority, but Lenin, more adept at personal diplomacy, attempted to mediate the conflict. He had need of both men and gained Trotsky's grudging consent to the special powers that Stalin demanded, with the tacit understanding that Voroshilov and his associates would respect the chain of command. The truce, though precarious, was aided by the Tenth Army's successful summer offensive against the forces of the Don Cossack leader, Peter Krasnov. In the fall Stalin made two trips to Moscow to discuss the military situation with Lenin. He returned to Tsaritsyn on October 11 as Krasnov made a final attempt to seize the city. Harried by insubordination, which he ascribed to Stalin, Trotsky telegraphed Lenin insisting on Stalin's recall and threatening to court-martial Voroshilov. By this time the siege had been lifted, thus furnishing a point of departure for the Stalinist legend of Tsaritsyn as the "Red Verdun" and one of the keys to the Bolshevik victory in the civil war.

Trotsky had his way, and Stalin was recalled to Moscow on October 19. The president of the Republic, Sverdlov, was sent to escort him on a special train, thereby concealing the reprimand with ceremonial honors befitting a conquering hero. Sverdlov arranged a meeting between the two antagonists, and according to Trotsky's account Stalin asked in a tone of exaggerated subservience, "Do you really want to dismiss all of them? They're fine boys." The answer was typical of Trotsky's brusque manner: "Those fine boys will ruin the Revolution, which can't wait for them to grow up." [14]

After consultation with Lenin, Trotsky proposed that Stalin be made a member of the special five-man Council of Defense. The new committee was established on November 30 and gave Stalin an outlet for his criticisms of the war effort without, as Trotsky put it, "wetting the powder of the War Department." Stalin's intrigues continued, however, and in December Trotsky transferred Voroshilov to the Ukraine.

Lenin valued Stalin's services as a military trouble-shooter far too much to accept Trotsky's complaints without reservation. Late in December, when the northern army of Admiral Alexander Kolchak captured Perm (later Molotov) in the western foothills of the Urals, Stalin was assigned the task of investigating the defending Third Red Army. Together with Felix Dzerzhinsky, the head of the Cheka, he arrived at the nearby city of Vyatka on January 5, 1919, and eventually prepared for Lenin a crisp and laconic analysis of the debacle. Unlike the torpid prose of his speeches and published articles, his confidential reports were models of clarity and precision. The disparity between the public and private Stalin points to a deeply rooted sense of inadequacy before a mass audience. His other traits—secretiveness, suspiciousness, and taciturnity—furnish additional clues to a personality that, if not misanthropic, lacked inner warmth toward human beings as individuals. Yet his gifts as an administrator and political technician were remarkable. In a democratic society his aspirations toward political power would have been thwarted by the necessity of gaining a popular mandate; in Soviet Russia the party machinery came to serve as a substitute for the electoral process.

There were several concealed barbs for Trotsky in Stalin's reports on the Third Army. The war commissar conceded, in answer to Lenin's plea for a reconciliation between the two, that "Compromise is of course necessary, but not a rotten one. . . . I consider Stalin's patronage of the Tsaritsyn tendency a most dangerous ulcer." According to Trotsky's uncorroborated version, Stalin was then dispatched to the southern front but again recalled for insubordination: "He came back sheepish but apparently not resentful." [15] Declining a new military assignment, he remained in Moscow several months. In March he married for the second time. His bride, apparently already his mistress, was the young Nadezhda Alliluyeva, twenty-two years his junior and usually described as a "beauty" by those who knew her. The couple lived in a small and unpretentious house—former servants' quarters—within the Kremlin walls.

Stalin had little time for domesticity. On March 30, less than a week after his marriage, he was chosen People's Commissar of State Control. This new department—renamed the Workers' and Peasants' Inspectorate in 1920—was designed to combat the evils of bureaucracy by creating a kind of super watchdog over every branch of administrative machinery. Stalin's unofficial status as one of the party elite had been confirmed shortly before by his appointment to the newly formed Politburo (Political Bureau), nominally responsible to the Central Committee. He also became a member of the Orgburo (Organizational Bureau), charged with supervision of party personnel. With these three posts he combined the highest policy making decisions with drab but vital bureaucratic functions. His devotion to the minutiae of party business was considered most commendable by his colleagues, who scorned the tedium of paper shuffling and record keeping. As a master of party routine he was one day to master the party.

In May 1919 Stalin resumed his military inspections. In his usual efficient but peremptory manner, he supervised the defense of Petrograd against the White forces of General Nikolai Yudenich. In October he was sent to the southern front, where General Anton Denikin's troops threatened a breakthrough to Moscow. The collapse of the Denikin offensive soon afterward reflected credit on Stalin, although his efforts were overshadowed by Trotsky's spectacular feat in galvanizing the Seventh Red Army against a second attempt by Yudenich to seize Petrograd.

Except for final mopping up operations and a brief campaign in the Crimea in 1920, the civil war ended with the defeat of Denikin and Yudenich. Russia was prostrate, but the Communist regime was secure against its internal enemies. Externally, however, a resurgent Poland under Marshal Joseph Pilsudski posed a constant danger to the weak Soviet Republic. In the spring of 1920 Pilsudski launched an attack on the Ukraine. The Poles took Kiev, but their hostile reception by the Ukrainian peasantry and an effective counter-offensive by the Red Army forced Pilsudski's legions into headlong retreat. Stalin, assigned to the southwestern front as political commissar, publicly warned of the risks involved should the Red Army carry the fight to Polish soil. Disregarding his own sensible advice, he finally sided with Lenin in the Politburo's decision to order a march on Warsaw. The prospect of a Red Poland—and a bridgehead to Germany—was too tempting to resist.

By mid-August, General Mikhail Tukhachevsky had reached the gates of the Polish capital. But his reserves were too thin and his supply lines overextended. The Russians were thrown back in disarray. The southern army, under Stalin's political direction, had sought a share of the glory by advancing toward Lvov instead of reinforcing Tukhachevsky. Trotsky, who had opposed the Polish adventure from the first, was the only party leader to emerge from the episode with credit. Peace with Poland was signed in March 1921, a date marking the end of War Communism—that awkward blend of military necessity and Marxist dogma—and a strategic retreat toward capitalism with the introduction of the New Economic Policy.

CHAPTER IV

The Struggle for Power

THE RESTORATION OF PEACE AND THE ECONOMIC RECOVERY ASSO-
ciated with the New Economic Policy allowed the Soviet Republic a breathing spell for the first time in its short but crisis-ridden
history. The hierarchy in the Communist party (as it was now
officially called) had not changed substantially since the October
Revolution. Stalin was still virtually unknown to the general
public, but his self-confidence had vastly increased with the mul-
tiplication of his duties and the ruthless efficiency with which he
performed them. Outwardly his personality had scarcely altered.
Unlike Trotsky's air of haughty arrogance, he conducted himself
with modesty and circumspection. His patience and quiet affability concealed vanity and sensitivity, yet he impressed his associates as an able technician without the obvious flaw of a runaway
ego. Only with subordinates did he display those qualities of
rudeness, vulgarity, and sly cunning that were to appear more
prominently as his career progressed.

On April 3, 1922, Stalin was chosen for still another post—that
of general secretary of the Central Committee. He seemed ideal
for the position because of his familiarity with party business as
the connecting link between the Politburo and the Orgburo.
None of the other party leaders relished the drudgery of such a
job, nor did Lenin or Trotsky indicate the slightest opposition
despite the latter's recollection that Lenin complained forebod-
ingly, "That cook will concoct nothing but peppery dishes." [1]
The appointment was considered routine—simply a reorganization of the Secretariat—and the office subsequently became the
apex of the party structure because Stalin made it so. Assisted by
Molotov, Lazar Kaganovich, and Valerian Kuibyshev, the new
general secretary conducted a quiet purge in the provinces.
Within a year he had replaced thirty-seven of the fifty party secretaries within the Russian portion of the Soviet Republic, though
local party conferences duly "elected" the designated candidates.
But Moscow and Petrograd, the two most important bastions of

the party organization, remained temporarily beyond the reach of Stalin's political network.

Contrary to the impression conveyed by Trotsky and other anti-Stalinists, the future dictator was neither a party hack nor a dull mediocrity before he grasped the party machinery in 1922 and used it to crush the Opposition and consolidate his power. He was already so well entrenched in the *apparat* by 1919 that only a concerted attack by Lenin could have dislodged him. Trotsky might have done so had he possessed Stalin's canine appetite for power, but he lacked the jugular instinct of the true political animal; nor did he or any other Bolshevik perceive a danger from the lackluster Georgian until it was too late.

Lenin did, in fact, launch an attack on Stalin in 1923 when illness had already undermined his authority. The cause of their break was both personal and political. Ironically, their political differences arose from the Georgian question, a derivation in turn of the peculiar history of that Caucasian country during the civil war. A Menshevik government had maintained a precarious independence despite a succession of foreign occupation troops—German, Turkish, and British. In February 1920, anticipating a Soviet conquest of Transcaucasia, Moscow established a Caucasian Bureau headed by Stalin's old associate, Ordjonikidze. An invasion of Georgia was interrupted by the Polish war, and on May 7 the Soviet government acknowledged Georgian independence. Ordjonikidze, presumably following Stalin's orders, secretly renewed preparations for another attack timed to coincide with a Communist insurrection. The planned rebellion broke out in February 1921, and Red Army detachments promptly crossed the border, capturing Tiflis before the end of the month. The Politburo had been belatedly informed of the projected campaign. Lenin, who at first balked at the scheme, was reconciled by the accomplished fact and ordered Ordjonikidze, Moscow's new viceroy in Tiflis, to make every possible concession to the Georgian people.

Stalin spent the month of July 1921 in Tiflis and managed to alienate the local Communist leaders with his strictures against Georgian nationalism. His plan to unite Georgia with Armenia and Azerbaijan in a Transcaucasian federation received Lenin's blessing, but the Politburo did not take up the matter until the summer of 1922 in conjunction with a thorough constitutional reform. By this time Lenin had suffered the first in a series of arteriosclerotic strokes and remained inactive until early October.

His relations with Stalin during his convalescence were cordial, and he was inclined to dismiss Trotsky's criticism of Stalin's Georgian policy as prompted by personal spite.

When Lenin resumed work in his Kremlin office he began to look into the matter more closely. The Georgian Central Committee had meanwhile condemned Stalin's project as "premature" and dispatched Budu Mdivani to Moscow to plead their case. Lenin had already indicated in a letter to the Politburo that Stalin's proposed federal union of Soviet republics was not wholly satisfactory and that the general secretary had a "slight aspiration toward hurry." Stalin replied rather testily that "Comrade Lenin himself 'hurried' a little" and that his "hurriedness" would supply fuel to the advocates of independence.[2] On October 6 Lenin expressed his loathing of "Great Russian chauvinism," yet a week later he approved a compromise draft of the new constitution at a meeting of the Central Committee. Stalin considered himself vindicated, and the Georgian Central Committee sent an indignant protest to Bukharin, who was known to be sympathetic to the Georgian cause. The telegram so irritated Lenin that he reprimanded the Georgians for their "unseemly tone," their abuse of Ordjonikidze, and their failure to abide by the normal channels of party communication.

Stalin, bolstered by Lenin's crushing reply to the Georgian opposition, gave Ordjonikidze a free hand in purging the dissidents. The Georgian Central Committee was replaced by a pro-Russian group, and most of its leaders were eventually sent to Moscow. Compared to later excesses of the Stalin era, the purge was mild indeed. But Lenin was disturbed by various reports and exasperated by an incident in which the burly Ordjonikidze had struck the short and paunchy Mdivani. Late in November he appointed an investigating commission headed by Felix Dzerzhinsky, and its findings upheld the Stalin-Ordjonikidze policy.

On December 13 and 16 Lenin suffered new attacks that left him partially paralyzed. He managed, however, to dictate letters to his secretaries and to his wife Nadezhda Krupskaya. Stalin's nerves were apparently frayed by uncertainty about Lenin's intentions, and on the 22nd he telephoned Krupskaya and proceeded to abuse her with some choice and probably obscene invective for meddling in politics. According to one version, perhaps apocryphal, he threatened her: "If you don't behave yourself we'll get another widow for Lenin."[3] Because of Lenin's illness Krupskaya concealed Stalin's offensive outburst from her husband but wrote to Kamenev asking that he and Zinoviev protect her from "rude interference with my private life and from vile invectives and threats." Her plea seems to have gone unheeded, for the Politburo had delegated Stalin to perform the unpleasant task of isolating Lenin from political activity. Ostensibly this was done out of solicitude for the ailing leader, but there are grounds for suspecting that the party elite did not welcome interference from a political spectator, however distinguished.

Conscious of his failing powers, Lenin on December 24–26 dictated a memorandum regarding his successors which subsequently became known as his "Testament." He referred to Stalin and Trotsky as the "two most able leaders of the present Central Committee," a judgment that must have shocked the other members of the Politburo. As for Stalin, "having become general secretary, [he] has concentrated enormous power in his hands, and I am not sure that he always knows how to use that power with sufficient caution." It was a prescient remark, though if one were to use the wisdom of hindsight it would seem a fantastic understatement of the problem. But compared to his criticism of Trotsky, Zinoviev, Kamenev, and Bukharin it was hardly more than a gentle rebuke.

During the next few days Lenin received further information about the Georgian question which confirmed his growing uneasiness about Stalin. On December 30–31 he dictated an essay usually referred to as the "Letter on the National Question." He charged that the right of secession from the Soviet state used by the Politburo to justify its nationalities policy had proved an "empty piece of paper incapable of defending the non-Russian minorities from the inroads of that true Russian, the Great Russian chauvinist, who in reality is a scoundrel and a tyrant—the typical Russian bureaucrat." Stalin's "hastiness and administrative impulsiveness have played a fatal role," and he recommended "exemplary punishment" of Ordjonikidze for his attack on Mdivani and a reexamination of the Dzerzhinsky report on Georgia because of the "enormous number of incorrect and prejudiced judgments that are undoubtedly contained in it." "Stalin and Dzerzhinsky," he concluded, "must be held politically responsible for this truly Great Russian nationalist campaign." [4] For the time being the document remained secret, and Lenin took no action along the lines he had proposed.

On January 4, 1923, Lenin added a postscript to his "Testament" reflecting disillusion with his foremost disciple and suggesting that some knowledge of the abusive telephone call to his wife may have reached him:

> Stalin is too rude, and this fault, entirely supportable in relations among us Communists, becomes insupportable in the office of general secretary. Therefore I propose to the comrades to find a way to remove Stalin from that position and appoint another man who in all respects differs from Stalin only in superiority—namely, more patient, more loyal, more polite and attentive to comrades, less capricious, etc. This circumstance may seem an insignificant trifle, but I think that from the point of view of preventing a split and from the point of view of the relations between Stalin and Trotsky which I discussed above, it is not a trifle, or it is a trifle that may acquire decisive significance.

Lenin's condition appeared to improve during the next three months. Among his writings were two articles on the Workers' and Peasants' Inspectorate, a post that Stalin had relinquished in May 1922. The first was published in *Pravda* on January 23 and could not be construed as an attack on Stalin. The second, though it did not mention him, constituted a scorching indictment of the commissariat, including its past performance. Publication would have meant an open acknowledgement that Stalin no longer enjoyed Lenin's favor, and it was only after several weeks' delay and a decision by the Politburo that the article appeared in *Pravda* on March 4. The next day, having now heard the full story of Stalin's offensive conduct toward Krupskaya, Lenin dictated a letter to Stalin, with copies to Kamenev and Zinoviev:

Dear Comrade Stalin!
You permitted yourself a rude summons of my wife to the telephone and a rude reprimand of her. Despite the fact that she told you that she agreed to forget what was said, nevertheless Zinoviev and Kamenev heard about it from her. I have no intention to forget so easily that which is being done against me, and I need not stress here that I consider as directed against me that which is being done against my wife. I ask you, therefore, that you weigh carefully whether you are agreeable to retracting your words and apologizing or whether you prefer the severance of relations between us.

Sincerely,
Lenin[5]

On March 7 one of Lenin's secretaries handed the letter to Stalin personally, and he dictated an immediate apology.

The Georgian question still preyed on Lenin's mind, and he

asked Trotsky's help in a letter of March 5, 1923, that was communicated by telephone:

Dear Comrade Trotsky:
    I wish very much to ask you to take upon yourself the defense of the Georgian case in the Central Committee of the party. At present, the case is under the "persecution" of Stalin and Dzerzhinsky, and I cannot trust their impartiality. Quite the opposite. If you were to agree to undertake the defense, my mind would be at rest. If for some reason you cannot agree to do so, please return the entire *dossier* to me; I shall consider that a sign of refusal from you.
With best comradely greetings,
Lenin[6]

The next day he wrote to the Georgian opposition (with copies to Trotsky and Kamenev): "I am with you in this matter with all my heart. I am outraged at the rudeness of Ordjonikidze and the connivance of Stalin and Dzerzhinsky. I am preparing for you notes and a speech."

Trotsky received the Georgian material from one of Lenin's secretaries, who informed him that Lenin was "preparing a bombshell" for Stalin at the forthcoming party congress. But Lenin was permanently removed from the political scene on March 9 when a third major stroke incapacitated him. Trotsky, presented with an opportunity to crush Stalin—or at least to humiliate him—merely temporized. He arranged that "rotten compromise" which Lenin warned would be the result of any agreement with Stalin. He looked upon Zinoviev as his chief rival, and with Kamenev as an intermediary he had promised even before Lenin's relapse not to press the attack on Stalin if there was a "radical change in the policy on the national question, a discontinuance of persecutions of the Georgian opponents of Stalin, a discontinuance of the administrative oppression of the party, a firmer policy in matters of industrialization, and an honest cooperation in the higher centres." Stalin readily consented, for he had no other choice at the moment. When it became apparent that Lenin's recovery was doubtful, he moved closer to Zinoviev and Kamenev in a combination to stop Trotsky.

The epitome of amiable reasonableness, Stalin fit none of the stereotypes of the power-seeking politician—still less the image of monstrous tyranny that he was to project in the 1930's. If anyone was cast in the role of dictator, it was Trotsky. The enormous popularity of the vain and imperious war commissar reminded the party wheelhorses of the French Revolution. Would their revolution, too, succumb to a new Bonaparte? The triumvirate—Stalin, Zinoviev, and Kamenev—was probably not greatly worried, but rumors originating in the party center about Trotsky's Bonapartist tendencies swept the country.

The Twelfth Party Congress, delayed by Lenin's illness, met in April 1923. The preliminary arrangements included a farcical display of reluctance on the part of both Stalin and Trotsky to assume Lenin's mantle by presenting the political report of the Central Committee—in effect, the keynote address. Trotsky proposed that Stalin, as general secretary, deliver the report. Stalin replied that the party would not understand: "The report must be made by the most popular member of the Central Committee." Zinoviev then grasped the opportunity, but his speech was received with unaccustomed coolness. Stalin, it developed, had quietly gained the support or friendly neutrality of most of the delegates through his control of party patronage and the disciplinary powers of the Secretariat.

Stalin could have demonstrated his authority more impressively had he chosen. But he preferred to bide his time, to conciliate his opponents, and to invoke Lenin's name with humility and reverence. The Twelfth Congress may be said to have founded the cult of Lenin while the leader was still alive. Stalin's speeches displayed a new self-assurance and a colloquial style in debate that must have appealed to the provincial party members—for the most part "practicals" rather than intellectuals. Trotsky, abiding by the terms of his understanding with Stalin, raised no embarrassing questions and confined his major address to economic matters.

The congress accepted a few changes in the party organization as a gesture toward implementing Lenin's strictures on the evils of bureaucracy. The Central Committee was enlarged from twenty-seven to forty to bring in new blood, and the Central Control Commission—originally designed as an independent check on party officials—was increased from seven to fifty and its powers augmented. The latter became a Stalinist preserve under its new chairman, Kuibyshev, while most of the thirteen additional members of the Central Committee proved to be reliable Stalinists. The Secretariat emerged intact, though Zinoviev was aware of the problem and proposed in September 1923 to infiltrate Stalin's bastion by appointing Trotsky and another member of the Politburo to form a three-man collegium. The plan was broached at an informal meeting with Bukharin, Voroshilov, and others at a Caucasian resort, and Stalin countered with a compromise scheme. Trotsky, Zinoviev, and Bukharin would become members of the Orgburo and thus keep an eye on the administrative affairs of the party. Only Zinoviev took advantage of Stalin's concession, and finding nothing amiss, he ceased attending.

Troubled by a persistent fever during the fall and winter, Trotsky remained aloof from his would-be followers and reluctant to press an attack outside the Central Committee. On December 8, however, he published an oblique thrust at the party machine in *Pravda* which the triumvirate chose to exploit. After a preliminary offensive in the press, a party conference in January 1924 censured the Trotsky Opposition for factionalism and "petty-bourgeois deviation" from Communist principles. Stalin led the assault on Trotsky—"this patriarch of bureaucrats" who needed party democracy "as a hobbyhorse, as a strategic manoeuvre." [7]

Trotsky failed to attend the conference, having left for the warmer climate of the Black Sea on January 18. Three days later Lenin died, and the triumvirate moved quickly to nurture the Leninist cult with an imposing state funeral and the preservation of the corpse—eventually to be interred in an elaborate mausoleum on Red Square. Trotsky missed the funeral, according to his own account, because a telegram from Stalin deceived him about the date and urged that he continue his journey since it was impossible to return in time. His absence was disappointing to his followers and gratifying to his enemies, but his presence could scarcely have altered the balance of political power. Eulogies honoring the fallen leader filled the press, and Stalin's contribution, delivered at a memorial session of the Congress of Soviets, departed significantly from the traditional rhetoric of Bolshevism. Reflecting his seminary training, the speech was couched in the sacerdotal idiom of the Orthodox Church: "Departing from us, Comrade Lenin enjoined us to hold high and guard the purity of the great title of member of the party. We vow to you, Comrade Lenin, that we shall fulfill your behest with honor!" The reiterated refrain constituted a kind of revolutionary litany, and the speech became known as "Stalin's oath." However repugnant it would have sounded to Lenin himself, it represents a superb example of Stalin's instinct for the emotional and "primitive" in a doctrine whose intellectual purity Marx and Lenin had guarded with dedicated zeal.

The policy of isolating Trotsky and his followers gained momentum in 1924. Beginning in February new recruits to the party were admitted in unprecedented numbers—some 240,000 by the close of the "Lenin enrollment" at the end of May. Selected by Stalin's efficient apparatus, they diluted still further the ranks of the Opposition. During the same period "opportunists" and other undesirables, many suspected of political unreliability, were expelled from the party. In April the Commissariat of War, hitherto Trotsky's sanctuary, was violated by one of Zinoviev's disciples, Mikhail Frunze, who replaced Trotsky's faithful deputy, Efraim Sklyansky.

On the eve of the Thirteenth Party Congress in May, Stalin survived a mortifying and potentially dangerous episode when Lenin's "Testament" was read to a meeting of the Central Committee and a few selected delegates. Krupskaya had sent the document to Kamenev with a note expressing Lenin's wish that his comments be submitted after his death to the next party congress. "Terrible embarrassment paralyzed all those present," reports an eyewitness to the scene. "Stalin, sitting on the steps of the rostrum, looked small and miserable. I studied him closely. In spite of his self-control and show of calm, it was clearly evident that his fate was at stake." [8] Zinoviev and Kamenev, still under the delusion that Trotsky was the major enemy, extricated Stalin from possible oblivion by avowing that he had mended his ways and that Lenin's fears had not materialized. A motion to restrict the document to heads of delegations carried by thirty votes to ten. Approximately a week later Stalin made a formal offer to resign, and it was unanimously rejected by the Central Commtitee. No one, not even Trotsky, ventured to challenge the authority of the general secretary.

Trotsky remained passive during the party congress, and aside from a few minor sallies the political struggle was suspended until the fall. He again furnished the pretext for a new campaign by the triumvirate when he wrote an introduction to a volume of his collected articles and speeches of 1917. Entitled "Lessons of October," it recalled the "strikebreaking" tactics of Zinoviev and Kamenev on the eve of the Bolshevik Revolution and went on to compare Lenin's strategic genius on that occasion with the hesitant leadership that had led to the Communist debacle in Germany in 1923. The party was soon convulsed by a polemical brawl known under an elegant but inaccurate label as the "literary debate." By raking up past controversies Trotsky left himself open to an obvious and devastating riposte—his bitter disputes with Lenin, especially before 1914. Now that the Lenin mystique had taken a firm grip on the party, a few choice quotations made in the heat of ideological combat over a decade ago were enough to cast doubt on Trotsky's credentials as a true Leninist.

Stalin's major contribution to the quarrel was a speech made in November 1924 questioning the "legend about Trotsky's special role in the October uprising" and an analysis of "Trotskyism as a peculiar ideology that is incompatible with Leninism." From this point onward the writing of history—at least party history—became increasingly a political act and less a scholarly art. But the more flagrant perversions of the historical record were not perpetrated until the mid-thirties. Stalin could still admit that Trotsky "did, indeed, fight well in October," and even to refer to his own "mistaken position" in the spring of 1917. Neither concession would be politically tenable a few years later.

Trotsky was taken aback by the violence of the assault. Again he sought refuge in the dignity of silence, a tactic that had no prospect of success when his chief asset was his formidable skill as a dialectician. His fever also returned, a coincidence that suggests psychosomatic illness. Acknowledging his submission to the party but refusing to confess his "errors," he resigned as war commissar in January 1925. Stalin remained formally respectful toward his foe, speaking of "Comrade Trotsky" and blocking Zinoviev's and Kamenev's attempt to expel him from the Politburo. He appeared in the role of a moderate, a healer of the party's wounds and an opponent of vindictive measures against the Opposition. Perhaps it was not entirely a pose, for he had mastered the nuances of political guile better than the other triumvirs and sensed that drastic action against a still popular figure was premature. As he explained eleven months later, "We knew that the policy of amputation was fraught with great dangers for the Party, that . . . bloodletting—and they demanded blood—was dangerous, infectious: today you amputate one limb, tomorrow another, the day after tomorrow a third—what will we have left in the Party?" [9]

With Trotsky's defeat the troika, which had never been more than an alliance of convenience, began to disintegrate. Dissension would have come sooner had Trotsky refrained from his ill-timed attack on Zinoviev and Kamenev. The latter, as the weakest of the partners, lost control of the Moscow party organization to Stalin, and though he remained a member of the Politburo, it was as Zinoviev's auxiliary that he continued to participate in the political struggle. Zinoviev remained solidly entrenched as the party boss of Leningrad (as Petrograd had been named after Lenin's death). His presidency of the Communist International (Comintern) since its inception in 1919 was still a post of great prestige even though the prospects of world Communism had diminished considerably in the interim.

During the summer of 1925 Zinoviev cast about for a soft spot in Stalin's political armor. He found it, so he thought, in a doctrinal issue—the supposed deviation of the N.E.P. from Leninist orthodoxy. Assuming a vantage point on the Left, he attacked the pro-peasant policy of the party leadership as a retreat from socialism. In October, with Kamenev, Krupskaya, and Gregory Sokolnikov, the commissar of finance, he submitted the so-called "platform of the four" to the Central Committee calling for free debate within the party. The protest extracted a slight concession—a resolution on the agrarian question warning of the kulak danger, that is, the increasing influence of the well-to-do peasant as opposed to the proletariat and poor peasant.

When the Fourteenth Party Congress met in December 1925 Stalin's apparatus had packed the hall with "loyal" delegates, far outnumbering the Leningraders backing Zinoviev. The Opposition was nevertheless permitted to have its say—amid a running fire of heckling interruption—and Kamenev for the first time spoke boldly of the growing dictatorial power of the general secretary. "I have reached the conviction," he declared, "that Comrade Stalin cannot perform the function of unifier of the Bolshevik general staff. . . . We are against the doctrine of individual control; we are against the creation of a 'chief'." Following his usual custom, Stalin left the verbal pyrotechnics to his subordinates, retaining his low keyed and matter of fact approach in refuting the Opposition arguments. The debate, as if adhering to a preordained ritual, changed few if any minds. A moderate resolution backing the Stalinist line carried by 559 votes to 65.

The resounding victory for the official policy led to a purge of the Leningrad organization. In January 1926 Molotov, Stalin's faithful acolyte in the Secretariat, headed an impressive delegation to the former capital, and by intensive work in the party cells and the transfer of key officials it won over some ninety-six per cent of the local membership. Zinoviev was removed as chairman of the Leningrad Soviet and Kamenev demoted to candidate status in the Politburo. Stalin's "collective" leadership was insured by the election of three of his supporters—Molotov, Voroshilov, and Mikhail Kalinin—to the party's ruling body.

Trotsky remained contemptuously aloof from the struggle between Stalin and Zinoviev. Only in the spring of 1926 did he respond to the overtures of his former enemies. Kamenev told

Trotsky that it would be "enough for you and Zinoviev to appear on the same platform, and the party will find its true Central Committee." [10] The illusion thus persisted that personalities and speeches could prevail against the party machinery. Stalin's opponents continued to underestimate him because they could neither respect nor understand him. In accepting the easy premise of his intellectual inferiority as if it were a debilitating political handicap, they explained his success as an unsavory compound of fraud, deceit, and cunning. Their judgment was not wholly wrong—such stratagems were certainly part of Stalin's repertoire —but they were outmaneuvered at every turn by a master tactician who combined the skills of a superior administrator with the shrewd insight of a born politician. It was paradoxical that Russian nationalism—with a Marxist gloss—should have reasserted itself under the leadership of a Georgian revolutionary (just as French nationalism flourished under the Corsican Bonaparte and German nationalism found release in the Austrian Hitler). Yet of Stalin's major rivals—Trotsky, Zinoviev, Kamenev, and Bukharin—three were of Jewish origin and all were Westernized intellectuals whose rapport with the Russian masses was tenuous at best.

Stalin's theoretical equipment, though meager, was attuned to the harsh realities of Russian society and the limitations of abstract Marxism. His chief ideological crutch—"socialism in one country"—suited the needs of a party that had lost much of its missionary zeal following successive Communist defeats in Hungary, Poland, and Germany. Revolutionary romanticism gave way under Stalin to national self-interest and the conviction that backward Russia was not necessarily foredoomed to stagnation because the European proletariat had been seduced by the gaudy trappings of capitalist civilization. He therefore had a psychological advantage over Trotsky, whose theory of "permanent" or world revolution offended national pride by suggesting that Russia could not by herself achieve a Communist society.

The united Opposition that emerged in the summer of 1926 was reduced to a semi-conspiratorial existence. Totaling no more than 8,000 in a party approaching three-quarters of a million, the dissenters were hopelessly outnumbered. But they formed a resolute elite amid a flabby mass of opportunists, time-servers, and political spectators, just as Lenin's Bolsheviks had furnished the driving force for the revolutionary workers and soldiers in 1917. Unfortunately for the Opposition, it confronted not Kerensky's feeble Provisional Government but a formidable party machine molded in Stalin's image. In July, Zinoviev was dismissed from the Politburo, a move anticipating his loss of authority in the Comintern. The Opposition could have been given the *coup de grâce* without prolonging the agony, but Stalin sought to expose it as ideologically bankrupt in the eyes of his followers.

Growing desperate, the Opposition leaders tried to bring their message to the factory workers in person. Their audiences remained apathetic, however, as the disruptive tactics of party agents and supporters made it difficult even for Trotsky to obtain a hearing. Stalin obtained a virtual surrender in mid-October when his chief opponents confessed their breach of party discipline and promised to refrain from factional activity in the future. By thus humiliating himself Trotsky hoped to preserve some influence in the party. But he was quickly disillusioned when Stalin proceeded to ignore the "bargain" by preparing an attack on the Opposition at the forthcoming party conference. Outraged, he denounced Stalin to his face at a Politburo meeting on October 25, ending any further hope of compromise with an open insult: "The first secretary poses his candidature to the post of the grave-digger of the revolution!" [11] Stalin, white-faced, stalked from the room. The next day the Central Committee removed Trotsky from the Politburo, ousted Kamenev as a candidate member, and stripped Zinoviev of his Comintern functions.

The crushing defeat of the Opposition did not elevate Stalin to the status of dictator. The party tradition of collective leadership was still too firmly entrenched for undisguised one-man rule, nor could he rely upon an automatic majority in the Politburo. Only gradually, by almost imperceptible steps, did his usurpation of party prerogatives become apparent. And to the average cell member—docile, conscientious, and politically unsophisticated despite a veneer of Marxist indoctrination—it no doubt seemed appropriate that Stalin should take up the burdens that Lenin had laid down. Strong leadership was, after all, a Bolshevik tradition too, and few were able to equate Stalin's growing ascendancy with a fundamental change in the nature of the party.

Contrary to the party statutes, which required an annual congress, no such meeting was convened in 1926. Anticipating a final disposition of the Opposition question, Stalin delayed calling the Fifteenth Congress until December 1927. Shortly before, Trotsky and Zinoviev had been expelled from the party for organizing protest demonstrations in Moscow and Leningrad in conjunction with the official celebration of the tenth anniversary of the October Revolution. The Fifteenth Congress confirmed the expulsions and added more than ninety other leading dissidents to the list of excommunicates. Of the prominent anti-Stalinists only Kamenev was allowed to speak, and his contribution, a confession of failure and a plea for mercy, aroused only jeering scorn. Stalin set the tone by pronouncing it the "most lying, hypocritical, fraudulent and scoundrelly of all the opposition speeches delivered here." [12]

Thoroughly humbled, Zinoviev and Kamenev promptly recanted and were eventually readmitted to the party. Trotsky refused to abase himself, and in January 1928 he was deported to Alma Ata in Central Asia. Thirteen months later he was exiled from the Soviet Union. Unprepared as yet to deal with his party enemies in a ruthless fashion, Stalin exercised what would later seem unusual compassion. In 1940, however, one of his agents penetrated Trotsky's retreat near Mexico City and accomplished by assassination what would have seemed an impolitic solution in 1929.

Hardly had the so-called Left Opposition been shattered when Stalin was confronted by a new set of opponents in the Politburo. This Right Opposition, as it came to be labeled, was led by Bukharin, Alexei Rykov, the titular president of the Soviet Union, and Mikhail Tomsky, the chief of the trade unions. The quarrel was occasioned by Stalin's sudden turn to the Left, a shift brought on by economic necessity rather than ideological conviction. The nagging agrarian problem entered a more acute phase early in 1928 as a grain shortage threatened the towns and cities with famine. Crop failures had heightened the emergency, but the basic difficulty lay in the shaky structure of Soviet agriculture. Land holdings had been fragmented as a result of the Bolshevik Revolution, and the peasants, who consumed most of their own produce, were reluctant to sell their meager surplus to the state for prices that would buy few consumer goods.

On January 15, 1928, Stalin and Molotov departed on a three week tour of inspection in western Siberia, an area largely unaffected by drought. Upon their return the government struck hard at peasant grain hoarders, though the operation was camouflaged as a drive against kulaks and speculators. Stalin admitted that the emergency brought with it "arbitrary administrative measures, the infringements of revolutionary law, the house-to-house visitations, the unlawful searches and so on." [13] In view of the excesses that were to follow, Stalin's squeamishness about these minor acts of illegality seems almost ludicrous. Rumors spread that the N.E.P. would be abandoned for the stringent economic policies of the civil war era. Stalin quickly denounced such talk as "counter-revolutionary chatter," but in the spring he was forced to admit that a small scale peasant economy offered no permanent solution to Russia's agrarian ills. "The way out," he declared, "lies, above all, in passing from small, backward and scattered peasant farms to united, large socially-conducted farms, equipped with machinery, armed with scientific knowledge and capable of producing the maximum amount of marketable grain."

During the first months of 1928 Rykov proved the most outspoken critic in the Politburo of Stalin's agricultural policy. In June, as the grain crisis deepened, Bukharin openly joined him; and with the support of Tomsky and the tacit approval of Kalinin and Voroshilov the Right Opposition appeared to have a working majority in the top party organ. But within a few weeks they were forced to admit that victory had eluded them. On July 11, in a personal meeting with his former enemy Kamenev, Bukharin inveighed against Stalin as a "Genghis Khan," an "unprincipled intriguer who subordinates everything to his appetite for power." Kalinin and Voroshilov had defected at the last minute: "Stalin," complained Bukharin, "has some special hold on them." 14

In the interest of party solidarity, both Stalin and Bukharin denied reports of a split in the Politburo. The general secretary, as was his custom, prepared for the attack by launching sorties on the flank. In November 1928 the Moscow party organization was purged of Bukharin supporters, and in December at the eighth Congress of Trade Unions, Tomsky was in effect stripped of his power as the Soviet labor boss. Stalin began a direct assault against the "Right deviation" at a Central Committee meeting in April 1929. Bukharin's "secret negotiations with Kamenev's group" was made to seem a "flagrant expression of . . . disloyalty and factionalism," and his errors on the agrarian question were recited at length. The Central Committee obediently passed a resolution of censure against Bukharin and his two colleagues, although the document was temporarily withheld from public circulation. In July, Bukharin was deprived of the presidency of the Comintern, a post he had inherited from Zinoviev in 1926. He lost his seat in the Politburo in November amid a torrent of abuse in the party press. After an abject confession of their misdeeds, the trio of penitents was allowed to remain in the party. Rykov, in fact, retained his Politburo membership for another year, but by the end of 1929 the Bolshevik party had been thoroughly cowed by its general secretary.

CHAPTER V

Russia's Iron Age

THE YEAR 1929 WAS AN IMPORTANT DATE IN BOTH RUSSIAN AND world history. For the industrialized West it marked the beginning of the Great Depression, an economic crisis that Communists, poring over the Marxist canon, had long predicted in apocalyptic but largely theoretical terms. Yet when the collapse—or, rather, paralyzing debilitation—of the capitalist system actually came, it proved as unexpected to the dogmatists of the Comintern and the Kremlin as the demise of Tsardom had to professional revolutionaries in 1917.

For Russia, 1929 was not only the inaugural year of Stalin's dictatorship; it also produced a trauma of the social order no less profound than that induced by a major depression. But instead of idle factories, mass unemployment, and price deflation, the chronic ills of a free market economy in its downward cycle, the Soviet leaders decreed a "second Russian Revolution" to collectivize the farms and expand the industrial facilities of the nation. It was to be a bold and unprecedented attempt to "socialize" a backward and largely agrarian economy by forced draft—to encompass in a single decade the nineteenth-century industrial revolution of the Western world.

Stalin's emergence as a "super-industrializer" was an impromptu performance, for he had consistently ridiculed political opponents for their grandiose schemes of economic expansion. He had allegedly dismissed a hydroelectric power project on the Dnieper River—subsequently completed with much fanfare in 1932—as the equivalent of a peasant buying a phonograph instead of a cow. Early in 1931 he delivered the classic rationale for his Five Year Plan while thoroughly immersed in a phantasmagoria of capital investment, production quotas, and statistical indices. "To slacken the tempo [of the Plan] would mean falling behind," he told a conference of industrial managers and technical personnel.

Those who fall behind get beaten. . . . One feature of the history of old Russia was the continual beatings she suffered because of her backwardness. She was beaten by the Mongol khans. She was beaten by the Turkish beys. She was beaten by the Swedish feudal lords. She was beaten by the Polish and Lithuanian gentry. She was beaten by the British and French capitalists. She was beaten by the Japanese barons. All beat her—because of her backwardness, because of her military backwardness, cultural backwardness, political backwardness, industrial backwardness, agricultural backwardness. They beat her because to do so was profitable and could be done with impunity. . . . Such is the law of the exploiters—to beat the backward and the weak. It is the jungle law of capitalism. . . . We are fifty or a hundred years behind the advanced countries. We must make good this distance within ten years. Either we do it, or we shall go under.[1]

Quite aside from Stalin's shrewd appeal to the patriotism of his audience, his version of the Tsarist past—Russia as a victim rather than an initiator of aggression—hardly squared with orthodox Marxist doctrine. It portended a fundamental revision of the party line on the cultural front. But for the moment Stalin was too deeply engrossed in his extravagant projections of Russia's economic future to bother with the task of ideological reconstruction.

Preliminary measures to curb the acquisitive instincts of the peasantry had meanwhile erupted into a massive drive to liquidate the kulaks as a class. Just as the Five Year Plan acquired a momentum that exceeded economic reality, so the original decision to collectivize the farms was grossly inflated by bureaucratic fantasy. The initial success of collectivization among the poor peasants encouraged Stalin to extend his program to the whole countryside. By March 1930 over half the twenty-five million peasant households had been brought into the collectives, a phenominal record achieved at the cost of agrarian chaos and civil war in the villages. In sullen defiance, the kulaks as well as many less prosperous *muzhiks* burned their crops, slaughtered their livestock, and destroyed their farm equipment. It was sabotage on a staggering scale that left famine in its wake. Millions of peasants were deported to inhospitable lands in Siberia, while the more recalcitrant, especially those offering armed resistance, were shot or sentenced to forced labor camps. There is no way of estimating the number who perished by hunger, privation, and execution, but Stalin's agricultural revolution was probably the greatest man made holocaust in modern times with the exception of the two world wars and Hitler's extermination of the Jews. A decade later Stalin privately admitted that a "terrible struggle" had taken place in which ten million kulaks (loosely defined) had been dispossessed of their individual holdings: "It was all very bad and difficult—but necessary." The "great bulk" of them were "very unpopular," he maintained, and were "wiped out by their labourers" [2]—evidently a euphemism for both government and vigilante action that exterminated an untold number of the most industrious and prosperous peasants.

Stalin himself called a halt to the collectivization frenzy on March 2, 1930, with a declaration in the press entitled "Dizzy with Success," a scornful indictment of those party workers whose enthusiasm had outrun common sense. "How could there have arisen in our midst such blockheaded exercises in 'socialization,' " he scolded, "such ludicrous attempts to overleap oneself, attempts which aim at bypassing classes and the class struggle, and which in fact bring grist to the mill of our class enemies?" Neglecting to mention whose orders had fanned their excessive zeal, he thus posed as a leader of moderation betrayed by incompetent subordinates.

The party had clearly overreached itself, and within two months some nine million peasant households were permitted to withdraw from the collectives. It was a strategic retreat reminiscent of the transition from War Communism to the N.E.P., but the respite was less prolonged. The collective farms were made more attractive by a variety of economic inducements. The most compelling incentives allowed the peasants to retain their homes, garden plots, household tools, and a few domestic animals. Their taxes were also lower, and for modest fees the government's machine-tractor stations eventually provided mechanized equipment to replace the eight million horses that had been butchered. By the close of 1932 the number of collective farmers was approximately the same as that achieved by compulsion in 1930. Private farming was virtually eliminated by the end of the decade. Stalin conquered the peasant, although the cost was heavy in terms of human suffering, social disorganization, and low agricultural productivity. Yet the ultimate objectives of the regime—the suppression of the "kulak danger" and the creation of a potentially more efficient method of farming—were successfully accomplished, unfortunately by methods that augured ill for a return to the "liberalism" of Lenin's day.

Stalin survived the first great crisis of his dictatorship with outward calm and an unflinching conviction that he had chosen the correct path. His demeanor and political audacity were all the more impressive because he was at the same time engaged in a gamble hardly less serious than his resolve to "socialize" agriculture—industrialization by government decree. The Five Year Plan had begun officially on October 1, 1928, and the original goals were both modest and reasonable. The limited capitalism of the N.E.P. was uncongenial to most party leaders, steeped as they were in the Marxist classics, and on doctrinal grounds there were no regrets that the "socialist offensive" had been resumed. But no one, including Stalin, had foreseen the frantic haste and drastic measures with which industrialization—or, indeed, collectivization—would be pushed, and as the tempo of the Five Year Plan accelerated beyond the realm of sober reality grumbling was heard in the highest reaches of the party.

Stalin's slogan that there were no fortresses which Bolsheviks could not conquer epitomized the enthusiasm with which many party members—and even ordinary workers—embarked upon a monumental task best described as "primitive socialist accumulation." Lacking surplus capital for anything but the most minimal investment program, the government deliberately lowered the living standard of the Russian people to the subsistence level. "Voluntary" industrialization loans and grain exports—at a time of severe domestic shortages and at prices reflecting the depressed world market—provided additional sources of capital investment. The production of consumer goods gave way to heavy industry—steel, coal, oil, hydroelectric power, and machine tools. Once the basic framework of an industrialized nation had been erected the rash promises about a socialist utopia might then be partially redeemed. To sustain the morale of this newly created labor force of skilled workers, administrators, technicians, and engineers proved all but impossible. The difficulties seemed insurmountable: low wages and a growing inequality of payment; chronic shortages of food, raw materials, and trained manpower; hardships, accidents, waste, and bureaucratic mismanagement; and eventually purges of managers and technical personnel for "sabotage," "wrecking," or suspected political disloyalty. No wonder an American worker at the great industrial complex in Magnitogorsk could write plausibly, "I would wager that Russia's battle of ferrous metallurgy alone involved more casualties than the battle of the Marne." [3]

Despite the inflated goals—a near doubling of production quotas set in 1928—the Five Year Plan was declared fulfilled at the end of 1932 in four and a quarter years. Although party propaganda and statistical legerdemain combined to conceal setbacks and blunders, the inaugural Plan and its successors represented an impressive achievement. Within a few years Russia became a great industrial power, and much of the credit inevitably accrued to Stalin. A more humane and democratic leader would have recoiled at the appalling hardships his draconian regime levied on the people. But there is no indication that he thought of the population in anything but abstract terms. All problems were exercises in political mechanics, and he became confirmed in his belief that the manipulation of the masses was simply the proper application of persuasion and compulsion. It has been said that he used barbarous methods to drive barbarism from Russia, a more sophisticated way of intimating that the end may justify the means. Perhaps the Soviet Union's defeat of Nazi Germany in World War II was the ultimate justification for his unique brand of tyranny.

Of Stalin the man, nothing but conjecture can be gleaned from the public record of the early thirties. From other sources it is possible to obtain a few intimate glimpses, but the only one of consequence involves the death of his second wife, Nadezhda Alliluyeva. An exemplary wife and mother—Vasily and Svetlana had been born of the marriage—Nadezhda's beauty had faded rapidly, and Stalin was hardly an attentive husband even when the pressure of duties allowed time for domesticity. In November 1932, shortly after the fifteenth anniversary of the October Revolution, the couple were guests at a party given in the Voroshilov's Kremlin apartment. According to the version circulated in the West for many years,[4] Nadezhda spoke bitterly of the excesses accompanying collectivization, a subject she had been brooding over for some time. Enraged and apparently under the influence of alcohol, Stalin cursed her obscenely and she fled to her own home. A few hours later she shot herself. Recent and apparently more reliable information indicates that the incident itself had no political implications.[5] Stalin is said to have called, "Hey you, have a drink!" and Nadezhda screamed, "Don't you dare 'hey' me!" and left the table. A servant found her body the next morning in her bedroom. A brief official announcement gave no hint of suicide, and rumors ascribed her death to appendicitis.

The tragedy shook Stalin badly. He had "sporadic fits of rage," and his suspicious temperament could never banish the thought that someone had put her up to it. His feeling was reinforced by a letter that Nadezhda left, "full of reproaches and accusations" about political as well as personal matters. It seems likely that his wife's suicide blew a psychological safety valve that had kept his morbid impulses in check. Henceforth he would trust no one: family friends and political comrades were all capable of treachery and deceit. He is reported to have offered his resignation at a meeting of the Politburo. His colleagues were acutely embarrassed, for no one had the temerity to suggest that perhaps it might be best that he step down. At last Molotov broke the awkward silence: "Stop it, stop it. You have the party's confidence." [6] The episode was closed, and the general secretary gave no further sign (until the outbreak of war nearly a decade later) that he had lost his composure or self-assurance.

The transformation of the Soviet economy by the three Five Year Plans of the pre-war era was accompanied by another facet of the Stalinist revolution: the remolding of Soviet society and ideology. Marxism-Leninism remained the official guideline, but one may speculate with reasonable assurance that the founding fathers of Communism would have been taken aback by Stalin's unique interpretation of their doctrine. It can be effectively argued that Stalinism was not the sum total of the personal whims of the Soviet dictator and that mass illiteracy and technical backwardness conditioned his response to the immense power he wielded so recklessly. Yet it was Stalin and Stalin alone who made the basic decisions. No other despot in modern times—even Adolf Hitler—has had the power and the will to alter so fundamentally the cultural and social fabric of his nation. The view that Stalin constructed a totalitarian state purely for his own political aggrandizement is possible but unlikely. He was, to be sure, pathologically suspicious of dissent and opposition, conduct that was soon to be equated with treason. And this required all the accouterment of a police state, a subject that will be examined in the context of the Great Purge. But Stalin, in his own perverted way, was an idealist. An ordinary dictator, one who seizes and retains power for personal ends, is content with the status quo. A doctrinaire idealist with unlimited power may become a dangerous fanatic or a revolutionary reformer. Stalin combined both traits in his person. He sincerely believed that the good society—Communist by definition—could be brought about by a monolithic party whose chief function was to enlist the masses in a collective enterprise. Those who declined or failed to participate were automatically suspect. Even the intellectuals, a politically harmless but influential elite, were obliged to toe the party line.

To his credit, Stalin gave top priority to raising the abysmally low educational level of the Russian people. He needed a literate population for the complex tasks of an industrial society, and in 1930 a majority of the peasants—still the largest single class—

could not command the simplest skills of reading and writing. Stalin boasted that the introduction of compulsory elementary education had raised the level of literacy from sixty-seven per cent of the population at the end of 1930 to ninety per cent at the end of 1933. His claim was grossly exaggerated, but within another decade the academic achievement of the average citizen under fifty closely approached that of the comparable age group in Western nations. Opportunities in higher education and a wide variety of vocational and technical schools were probably superior to those offered in other industrial countries. Skeptics might argue that the schools were the basic indoctrination unit of the Communist system, but the chance for advancement on individual merit was far greater under Stalin than it had been under the tsars.

"Socialist competition" was Stalin's watchword in the 1930's, and in practice he repudiated the egalitarian notions of the Marxist tradition as well as the nostalgic variations on the same theme that Lenin had advanced even after 1917. In general, the new privileged class of technicians and administrators earned its status by ability and education rather than the time-honored method of property ownership. Inequality of income did not repudiate Marx's teachings, Stalin argued, because no one could exploit another's labor as long as the means of production were not privately owned. The point is well taken if we accept the premise that the state cannot also become an instrument of exploitation, certainly an unwarranted assumption in the case of Stalin's Russia and other totalitarian countries. But some form of economic discrimination was obviously necessary to develop a skilled labor force from the peasant masses. The government added psychological incentives to material rewards, and "heroes of socialist labor" became glamorous figures akin to athletes and entertainers in the United States.

The Soviet citizen received tangible benefits to offset low wages, strict labor discipline, rationing, and other repugnant features of a regimented society. Perhaps most important, he was assured of a job at a time when mass unemployment was endemic to the capitalist West. Free medical treatment, retirement pensions, low rent, paid vacations, and lesser privileges added to the "socialized wage." The equality of women, the unattained goal of Western feminists, came close to reality under Stalin. Sexual mores, on the other hand, became more austere. "Free love" was frowned upon, and prostitution was severely repressed. The family assumed a new importance in Soviet life, with medals and special privileges for mothers who bore more than six children. Divorce was no longer granted automatically, and abortions were declared illegal except for medical reasons.

In matters of culture Stalin was a thorough philistine, though he took pride in the generous government support lavished upon educational and cultural activities. In such esoteric pursuits as chess and the ballet he was content to play the role of benign patron. But in scholarship, literature, and the arts the dead hand of political conformity, intellectual sterility, and artistic mediocrity strangled the promising developments of the 1920's. Paradoxically, Stalin was by no means anti-intellectual despite his disdain for the creative intelligentsia. He had a profound respect for knowledge, particularly science in its more practical aspects, and was something of an evangelist in his desire to uplift the masses to appreciate the best in art and literature. The result, however, was precisely the opposite—the vulgarization of culture to "educate" and guide popular taste.

To paint a picture or to write a novel was less an aesthetic than a political act. Writers and artists were shock troops in the construction of a new society, and Stalin demanded that their work be couched in the idiom of "socialist realism." Dramatists and novelists were told, in effect, to write inspirational tracts with simple plots, noble Communist heroes, and dastardly "White Guard" or Trotskyite villains. By no means all creative writing degenerated to this stereotyped level, but by the late thirties Soviet literature had become a slightly disguised branch of political propaganda.

The withering blight of Stalinism was somewhat less pronounced in the fine arts, for painting, sculpture, architecture, and music were more difficult to evaluate by ideological standards. Good painting, to Stalin, was essentially poster art—a true-to-life representation of Soviet workers or a historical tableau in which he was depicted (perhaps with other party leaders) as a handsome and commanding personality. Impressionism, abstracts, and other schools of modern painting were taboo as not readily comprehensible to the masses. Sculpture was likewise used to extol the positive features of the Soviet regime. Architecture, the least recondite of the arts, offered a magnificent opportunity to demonstrate the imagination and daring of a new society. But Stalin preferred massive grandeur to originality, and his conception of good taste hardly differed from that of a conventional bourgeois citizen of the nineteenth century. His public buildings were impressive to the untrained eye, yet their neo-baroque opulence was as banal as the pseudo-Gothic style that once dominated collegiate and church architecture in the United States. Melodic and easily understood music won Stalin's stamp of approval—tunes that he could whistle, according to his critics. Nevertheless, he tolerated and even enjoyed some types of classical music and drew the line only at dissonant and polyphonic orchestral compositions.

Among traditional academic disciplines, science was ordinarily exempt from party controls because of the absence of political content. The major exception was biology. By the late thirties Stalin chose to back the curious theories of Trofim Lysenko, a self-taught botanist whose belief in the inheritance of acquired characteristics challenged the orthodox school of Mendelian genetics. Stalin had little or no training in science, and his ludicrous attempt to establish an official school of biology derived in part from his faith in the perfectibility of mankind under socialism, a possibility that "bourgeois" genetics seemed to deny. The leading Soviet geneticist, Nikolai Vavilov, was arrested and perished in a labor camp in 1943.

The related field of psychology suffered under milder but no less objectionable political interference. The physiological school of psychology founded by Ivan Pavlov, renowned for his theory of the "conditioned reflex," was favored by the party as more appropriate to a materialist philosophy. Other approaches were therefore neglected, if not discouraged, and the psychoanalytic theories of Sigmund Freud were singled out for special condemnation.

The freedom and prestige of the social sciences were infinitely more precarious than the "pure" sciences, and in this area one could hardly say that independent scholarly investigation in the Western sense truly existed under Stalin. All political, economic, and social analysis was sifted through the ideological hopper of Marxism-Leninism-Stalinism. History, which had all but disappeared as a separate discipline in the academic curriculum, was revived in the early thirties as the intellectual spearhead of a revived Russian nationalism. A few eminent "bourgeois" historians had been allowed to publish during the twenties, but the de facto commissar of historical studies, Mikhail Pokrovsky, maintained unceasing vigilance against anti-Marxist historical interpretation. Pokrovsky was at least a professional historian rather than a party hack, though his depersonalized and abstract brand of Marxism portrayed Tsarist history as a gloomy chronicle of poverty, oppression, and imperialism. His death in 1932 was well timed, for he was posthumously denounced along with his followers.

Stalin took a personal interest in historical studies, and, if not a scholar, he fancied himself as something more than an amateur in the field of Russian history. In 1938 he was to confer his imprimatur on the notorious "short course"—the official history of the Communist party. But his highhanded interference in historical matters was foreshadowed as early as 1931 when he sent a letter to the journal *Proletarskaya Revolyutsia* denouncing a hapless disciple of Pokrovsky as a "semi-Menshevik" and a "camouflaged Trotskyist." "The task of the editorial board," he peremptorily declared, was to "raise the questions concerning the history of Bolshevism to the proper level, to put the study of the history of our Party on scientific, Bolshevik lines, and to concentrate attention against the Trotskyist and all other falsifiers of the history of our Party, systematically tearing off their masks." [7] Under the pressure of contemporary historical events, notably the rise of Nazi Germany, he ordered the rehabilitation of the Russian past, if not the Tsarist regime itself. "Progressive" rulers such as Peter the Great (little more than a syphilitic tyrant to Pokrovsky) and Tsarist generals such as Suvorov and Kutuzov became national heroes. Stalin emerged as the climactic personality in Russian history—the revolutionary heir to the Marxist legacy and the strong father figure who would lead his people to greatness.

The ideological straitjacket that Stalin designed for his new society might have remained simply an obnoxious and self-defeating example of cultural vigilantism had he been content with propaganda and other quasi-coercive methods of persuasion. But he became convinced by 1936 that dissent should be stamped out by force lest it destroy the intricate social fabric that he had labored so hard to fashion. Dissent, by the twisted logic of Stalinism, was equivalent to disloyalty and subversion. The creative as well as the political and technical intelligentsia was decimated in the orgy of bloodshed that followed.

CHAPTER VI

The Great Purge

ON DECEMBER 1, 1934, A YOUNG MAN NAMED LEONID NIKOLAYEV shot and killed Sergei Kirov, the powerful chief of the Leningrad party district and second only to Stalin in the ruling hierarchy. Seemingly the isolated act of an obscure fanatic, the assassination proved to be one of the great political crimes of modern history. It provided a pretext for Stalin's Great Purge—the liquidation of the Old Bolsheviks and the arrest of millions of Soviet citizens whose ultimate fate depended upon administrative caprice or the arbitrary decision of one man.

Stalin's reign of terror differed substantially from his brutal repression of the peasantry and lesser acts of illegality. For the first time he abandoned the Bolshevik tradition that the sword of the Revolution would be turned only upon "class enemies," never upon the party itself. The first significant departure from established procedure came when M. N. Ryutin, a prominent member of the Moscow party organization, circulated a lengthy anti-Stalinist program in 1932. Stalin called for the execution of the "Ryutin group," and since such summary treatment would have violated a party precedent, the Politburo and Central Committee looked into the affair. Stalin was shocked to discover that his "automatic" majority failed him in this instance. Kirov, hitherto a faithful Stalinist to all outward appearances, led the fight as a matter of "Leninist" principle. Ryutin and his associates were spared the death penalty; Stalin, humiliated by his first major rebuff since the subjugation of the Opposition in the twenties, is said to have sworn vengeance and prepared the groundwork for his subsequent purge.[1]

Kirov had no wish for a test of strength with Stalin. But he sensed the mood of the party—one of exhaustion from the frenetic pace of Stalin's economic revolution and disquiet at the barbaric practices that accompanied it. Assuming the stance of a moderate, at the Seventeenth Party Congress in January-February 1934—the "Congress of Victors" in the hyperbole of Soviet propaganda—he not only received an ovation that rivaled Stalin's but one as spontaneous as the other was contrived. On the surface the meeting appeared to be nothing more than a sounding board for the party chieftain. The speakers invariably offered appropriate verbal genuflections to the great Stalin, yet his authority was severely shaken behind the scenes: he was demoted by the Central Committee from *general secretary* to *secretary*. The shift in nomenclature was imperceptible to outsiders, but it signified that he no longer had complete control over the party Secretariat. He was forced to share power with three newcomers—Kirov, the most formidable of the trio, Kaganovich, and Andrei Zhdanov.

A period of relaxation followed the Seventeenth Congress. The harvest in the autumn of 1933 had been bountiful, ending the famine that had caused widespread starvation in the Ukraine, the central Volga region, and western Siberia. Former Oppositionists were reconciled and permitted to rejoin the party. The secret police (O.G.P.U.) was absorbed by the People's Commissariat of Internal Affairs (N.K.V.D.) and its power somewhat diminished, notably the right to pass death sentences. Genrikh Yagoda, who had been at odds with Stalin in the past, was placed in charge. In August 1934 a Writers' Congress sought to conciliate the intellectuals, and Bukharin (again in favor) and the famous novelist Maxim Gorky made a ringing plea for "proletarian humanism" before the assembled delegates. Further reforms were planned, especially a new constitution to replace the obsolete document of 1924. Kirov was the leading spirit behind the "policy of reconciliation," and he received the energetic support of Ordjonikidze and Kuibyshev (both former Stalin protégés) in forming a new majority in the Politburo.

Stalin took these checks on his authority as a personal affront but managed to conceal his anger under a surface amiability that had always been one of his distinguishing traits. Equally characteristic, he formulated a plan to crush his enemies and regain his accustomed place at the head of the party. As he is supposed to have told Kamenev and Dzerzhinsky in a rare moment of self-revelation in 1923, "To choose one's victim, to prepare one's plans minutely, to slake an implacable vengeance, and then to go to bed. . . . There is nothing sweeter in the world." [2] If the accuracy of the quotation cannot be confirmed, it nevertheless catches the flavor of the authentic Stalin. His personal secretariat, an elaborate organization headed by Alexander Poskrebyshev, had been expanded after the Ryutin affair to include a secret department for surveillance and liaison with the political police. Stalin's agents infiltrated the N.K.V.D. and eventually displaced the regular personnel. It was this secret apparatus that plotted Kirov's murder, although the details may never be known with certainty.

The assassin, Nikolayev, had been a party member of long standing but a social misfit whose personal problems he blamed upon the regime. Dismissed from his job as a guard at the Smolny Institute, the Leningrad party headquarters, he wrote long letters of complaint to various officials and came to the attention of Ivan Zaporozhets, the local deputy director of the N.K.V.D. The latter arranged an informal meeting with Nikolayev under an assumed identity. As an *agent provocateur* apparently acting under Stalin's orders (with the connivance of Yagoda), Zaporozhets skillfully channelled Nikolayev's hatred of the government bureaucracy toward a more personal object, namely Kirov. Later, probably in October 1934, Nikolayev gained access to Smolny but was apprehended with a pistol in his briefcase. Released by Zaporozhets, he made a second attempt on December 1 to negotiate Smolny's security cordon. This time the plan succeeded—most of the guards had been withdrawn—and Kirov was killed by a single shot as he stepped from his office into the corridor.

Stalin, Yagoda, and other party officials took a special train to Leningrad to conduct a personal investigation. A secret party directive issued on the evening of the assassination permitted the N.K.V.D. a free hand in the arrest and execution of alleged terrorists—that is, political suspects. The press created a crisis atmosphere with stories of numerous "White Guards" rounded up, implying that a vast anti-Soviet conspiracy aided by foreign nations lay behind the affair. Gossipers spread an even more fanciful tale that Nikolayev's motive was jealousy because his wife had been Kirov's mistress. On December 6, sixty-five "terrorists," all arrested prior to the assassination, were executed. Within two weeks another version of the plot was publicized: Nikolayev had been a member of the "Leningrad center" of Zinovievites, an organization to which the ubiquitous Trotsky was said to be linked. By the end of the month Nikolayev and thirteen of his "accomplices" were tried in secret and shot. Zinoviev and Kamenev, arrested in mid-December, were given a similar "trial" in January 1935. In return for a promise of leniency, they admitted political and moral responsibility for the murder while denying actual complicity in the crime. Zinoviev was sentenced to ten and Kamenev to five years in prison.

In his determination to purge the party of troublemakers—and it is a moot point whether he really believed in the "conspiracy" he had conjured up—Stalin did not neglect to tidy up his own trail to the Kirov affair. Members of the Leningrad N.K.V.D. with knowledge (or perhaps suspicion) of the circumstances were tried for negligence and given nominal prison terms which in practice amounted to sentences of honorable exile. They subsequently disappeared, however, in the Great Purge and were presumably shot. Only Zaporozhets seems to have survived these critical years, but his ultimate fate is unknown. Kirov's devoted bodyguard and attendant was killed in an automobile "accident" while being conducted to an interrogation the day after the assassination.[3] In an equally suspicious incident a few days later, Yagoda narrowly escaped injury when a truck crashed into his car and demolished it.

Zhdanov, a zealous apostle of party orthodoxy, took over Kirov's post and carried through a ruthless *chistka*—literally a "cleansing"—of party members and their families in the Leningrad area. Less drastic measures in other cities rid the party and the Komsomols (young Communist organizations) of unreliable or politically suspect elements. The purge was as yet a bloodless affair—many were simply reprimanded or expelled—but of the thousands deported to the desolate labor camps of northern Siberia a high proportion never returned. Stalin made no move against the "liberals" of the Politburo and Central Committee, although the convenient death of Kuibyshev, ostensibly of a heart attack, gave rise to rumors of foul play.

In the latter half of 1935 the moderate spirit of the "Kirov policy" appeared to have returned. Stalin went out of his way to portray himself as a kind and benevolent leader; and he was frequently photographed on ceremonial occasions handing out medals, accepting flowers from little girls, and other contrived performances to enhance his public image. Living standards made slow but steady gains, and food rationing, introduced in 1929, was finally abolished. In case the Soviet people had doubts that their lot had improved, Stalin solemnly assured them that "life has grown better, life has grown merrier." A special commission, with Stalin as chairman, labored on the new constitution and raised hopes for a new era of political leniency. Bukharin, as secretary of the commission, wrote the document with some assistance from Karl Radek. He took great pride in his handiwork, and on paper it was indeed the "most democratic constitution in the world"—to use the favored *agitprop* cliché. Stalin encouraged nationwide discussion of the draft constitution when it was submitted in June 1936, and according to official figures 527,000 meetings attended by 36,500,000 persons debated both the substance and the wording. Of the 154,000 amendments offered, only 43 alterations were made, most of them minor changes in phraseology. The constitution was formally accepted by the Congress of Soviets in December 1936, but it made no perceptible difference in the pattern of Stalin's dictatorship. The party ruled the government, and Stalin once again ruled the party with no indication that the "liberal" bloc in the Politburo had survived Kirov's death.

Whether real or simulated, Stalin's moderation came to an abrupt end several months before the introduction of the new constitution. On August 19, 1936, Zinoviev, Kamenev, and fourteen other Old Bolsheviks once associated with the opposition were charged with organizing a "terrorist center" under the leadership of the exiled Trotsky. It was the first of three sensational "show trials" that decimated the founders of the Soviet regime. At the lowest party level the purge had continued throughout 1935 and 1936. A new wave of expulsions and arrests followed a secret letter by the Central Committee of July 29, 1936, warning of counter-revolutionary plotters and calling for another screening of party members. Nevertheless, the "Trial of the Sixteen" opened an entirely new phase in Stalin's campaign to destroy his opponents. He now sought by confessions of guilt in open court to discredit them before the Russian public, and to a lesser extent to convince world opinion that a gigantic plot against the regime had been smashed.

All sixteen confessed (with some reservations by Ivan Smirnov) that since 1932 they had organized terrorist acts against Stalin and the Soviet leadership, of which the Kirov assassination had presumably been the only success. All were pronounced guilty and promptly shot. Since the testimony implicated Bukharin, Rykov, Tomsky, and others, the stage was set for the next trial. Anticipating his arrest, Tomsky committed suicide on August 24. But on September 10 *Pravda* surprisingly announced that an investigation had cleared Bukharin and Rykov, evidence that Stalin's original plan had gone awry. The setback had apparently arisen from a Central Committee or other top-level meeting at which Nikolai Yezhov, who had taken over Kirov's assignment in the party Secretariat, failed to convince the participants that a widespread conspiracy had been hatched. Bukharin spoke for three hours and is said to have denounced both Stalin and Yezhov: "Stalin's aim is to establish his personal power, to an unlimited extent, over the Party and the country. . . . That is why we are to be eliminated. But in order to eliminate us you [Yezhov] have had to resort to fraud, lies and provocation. . . . The Party and its Central Committee need to return to the traditions of Lenin and to call to order the police plotters who conceal themselves behind the authority of the Party. It is the NKVD, and not the Party, which today governs the country. It is the NKVD, and not the followers of Bukharin, which is preparing a *coup d'état*." [4] Stalin was then on vacation at the Black Sea resort of Sochi. On September 25 he and Zhdanov sent a telegram to the Politburo complaining that the secret police were "four years behind" in "unmasking the Trotskyite-Zinovievite bloc" and demanding that Yezhov be appointed to replace the incompetent Yagoda.[5] The appointment was quickly approved, and the *Yezhovshchina* that followed marked the extremity of Stalin's terror.

The second round of the Moscow trials began on January 23, 1937. The defendants, officially constituting the "Anti-Soviet Trotskyite Center," were Karl Radek, Deputy Commissar for Heavy Industry Yuri Pyatakov, the former ambassador to Britain Gregory Sokolnikov, and fourteen other party notables. The charges were expanded to include wrecking and sabotage as well as treasonable contact with German and Japanese agents to dismember the Soviet Union and restore Trotsky and his followers to power. Again the defendants confessed with elaborate and fanciful detail; four, including Radek and Sokolnikov, were sentenced to long prison terms and the others shot.

It is a reasonable assumption that many if not most of Stalin's associates had strong reservations about the necessity of the purge. But it took courage to express a doubt or to venture a protest, especially when dissent seemed not only futile but a sure road to prison or the firing squad. In its official pronouncements the Central Committee was forced to become an obedient claque, with its members offering proof of their loyalty and devotion to the party by abusing their former comrades and proclaiming the need for ever more stringent measures to safeguard the state from saboteurs and traitors. Yet there were a few who defied Stalin, at least to the extent of making unfavorable remarks on some aspect of his policy. One was Ordjonikidze, who had supported Kirov in 1934 and is said to have remained loyal to Pyatakov, his nominal subordinate in the Commissariat for Heavy Industry. According to the Soviet press, he died suddenly on February 18, 1937, of a "paralytic stroke" Almost twenty years later his onetime colleague, Nikita Khrushchev, declared that Ordjonikidze had been forced to shoot himself. At a Central Committee session beginning on February 23 a number of members protested the terror, perhaps the last time in Stalin's career that open criticism of the *Vozhd* (leader) was heard at a high-level party meeting. Many inarticulate (and probably inoffensive) delegates suffered with the "guilty." Khrushchev reported, perhaps with some exaggeration, that of the 139 members and candidates, 98 were later arrested and shot; many confessed to a variety of treasonable activity because of "cruel and inhuman tortures."

In the late spring and summer of 1937 Stalin turned his inquisitorial apparatus upon the armed forces. Although numerous theories have been advanced to explain his devastation of the officer corps, none are really satisfactory. As in the case of the major political victims, his underlying motive seems to have been a deep seated suspicion of treachery and a determination to make a clean sweep of any elements that might conceivably plot against his regime. The usual portents signaled the new purge, particularly the reintroduction of political commissars in the army. This system of dual military command had been used as a check on the loyalty of Red Army officers during the civil war and was later abandoned because of its obvious disruption of normal military discipline. Yan Gamarnik, chief of the army's Political Administration, was the first victim. On June 1 it was announced that he had become "involved with anti-Soviet elements" and had committed suicide. Ten days later a terse notice in *Pravda* revealed the arrest of five highly placed officers headed by Marshal Tukhachevsky, already a legendary hero of the civil war. Allegedly they had confessed to treasonable contact with foreign powers and were shot after a secret trial by a special military tribunal. The original charges were rather diffuse, but posthumous accusations included such specific crimes as espionage on behalf of Germany and Japan and collusion with Zinovievite-Trotskyite "terrorists" designed to overthrow the government. Evidence against Tukhachevsky, fabricated by the German Gestapo (perhaps in collaboration with the N.K.V.D.) and then "leaked" to Paris and Prague, played a minor role in the affair. Passed on to Stalin, who was not deceived as to its source and credibility, the Gestapo dossier furnished convincing "proof" to other Red Army commanders that the Tukhachevsky group had indeed been guilty.

The military purge next spread to the Far Eastern command of Marshal Vasily Blyukher, who had reportedly clashed with Stalin

in 1933 on collectivization policy and won special concessions for
the peasants in the eastern provinces. Blyukher lost a large proportion of his officers but was not displaced until 1938. He disappeared in silence, probably shot in November of that year. Silence, or at most a cryptic official notice, also characterized the
arrest or execution of thousands of army, navy, and air force officers, chiefly in 1937–1938. Estimates place the total number
purged at half the officer corps of about 70,000, including ninety
per cent of the generals and eighty per cent of the colonels.[6] The
morale and efficiency of the Red Army was seriously impaired,
though foreign intelligence estimates—and the politicians who
received them—tended to exaggerate its crippled condition. Soldiers and noncommissioned officers were not directly affected, and
the vacancies available to junior officers swiftly raised their rank
and status. In the long run, judging from the experience of
World War II, many of the new "Stalinist" generals performed
more ably than the older generation of civil war commanders
who survived the terror.

The last of the Moscow trials (March 2–13, 1938) furnished a
spectacular climax to the Great Purge, a kind of Grand Guignol
performance brought to life. The luminaries of the "Anti-Soviet
Bloc of Rights and Trotskyites" were Bukharin, Rykov, and Yagoda, and the supporting cast of culprits included Old Bolsheviks, a trio of physicians, and miscellaneous lesser offenders—
twenty-one in all. As at the other trials, the real defendant was
Trotsky, the evil genius whose subversive network had supposedly
penetrated the top levels of party and government. The usual
charges—and several new ones—were presented by the ex-
Menshevik prosecutor, Andrei Vyshinsky, and the usual confessions were made in open court. (One of the accused, the former
diplomat Nikolai Krestinsky, at first denied his guilt and then
reversed himself after another twenty-four hours in custody.) The
most bizarre feature of the trial was Yagoda's admission that he
had not only planned Kirov's murder—the third major version
presented by the Soviet authorities—but that with the help of the
three physicians on trial he had poisoned Maxim Gorky, Gorky's
son, Kuibyshev, and his former superior in the N.K.V.D., Vyacheslav Menzhinsky. Bukharin skillfully fenced with the prosecutor,
and by the use of Aesopian language—symbols, parables, and
double meanings—attempted to indict Stalin and proclaim his
own innocence. He flatly refused to admit that he had been the
agent of a foreign power or had plotted with Left Social Revolu-

tionaries to kill Lenin and Stalin as early as 1918. His fate was the same: death by shooting. Only three defendants escaped execution and were sentenced to long prison terms.

Other than the self-incrimination of the accused, the prosecution offered no convincing evidence at the Moscow trials of anti-Soviet activity. Nevertheless, the verdict was probably regarded as just by the great majority of ordinary Russians, who had no independent basis of judgment to counter the insistent barrage of government propaganda. Even outside Soviet jurisdiction, where opinion was theoretically formed on the merits of the case, no consensus was forthcoming. Moscow's anti-fascist policy was in the ascendancy, and many were inclined to give Stalin the benefit of the doubt since the defendents were linked specifically to Nazi Germany. Nor could the detailed confessions be ignored, for the accused bore no marks of violence. The answer as to *why* they confessed probably varies with each individual, but in general a combination of psychological and physical coercion was applied. A few resisted all pressure, including torture, and as risky subjects for public exhibition they were simply executed without fanfare.

The glare of publicity surrounding the "show trials" obscured the fate of anonymous millions—chiefly professionals, technicians, administrators, and party workers—sucked into the vortex of the Great Purge. Denunciations, both voluntary and forced, relationship by blood, marriage, or friendship to a suspect, routine investigation—such were the methods that filled the prisons and labor camps. Arrest quotas, ambitious police officials, mistaken identity, and other evils of a bureaucratic despotism nurtured the semi-autonomous empire of the N.K.V.D. An accurate breakdown of the number of arrests, sentences, and executions is impossible. Khrushchev revealed that in 1937–1938 Yezhov sent Stalin 383 lists containing the names of "many thousands" whose proposed punishment was to be approved.

Since the overwhelming majority of victims were innocent of any wrong doing, even by the grotesque standards of Stalinism, they were unable to comprehend the reason for their plight or to draw the necessary implications. Convinced that there had been a misunderstanding, they persisted in denying their guilt until "persuaded" to confess by prolonged interrogation, interrupted when necessary by less subtle methods. Not many, at least of the newly imprisoned, were able to associate their particular fate with the political system. Fewer still understood that Stalin himself had instigated the mass arrests. Party members, whose training had conditioned them to dogmatic certitude about the merits of the regime, displayed more naiveté than less privileged citizens. There is, for example, no more poignant commentary on these macabre times than this plea to Stalin sent by Robert Eikhe, a candidate member of the Politburo shot in 1940:

> I have not been guilty of even one of the things with which I am charged and my heart is clean of even the shadow of baseness. I have never in my life told you a word of falsehood and now, finding my two feet in the grave, I am also not lying. . . . I am asking and begging you that you again examine my case, and this not for the purpose of sparing me but in order to unmask the vile provocation which, like a snake, wound itself around many persons in a great degree due to my meanness and criminal slander. I have never betrayed you or the party. I know that I perish because of vile and mean work of the enemies of the party and of the people, who fabricated the provocation against me.[7]

Stalin spared neither friends nor relatives from his remorseless vendetta. Members of both the Svanidze and Alliluyev families suffered, and one of his oldest comrades, Abel Yenukidze, the secretary to the Central Executive Committee of the Congress of Soviets, was first humiliated and finally shot. His downfall is an instructive example of Stalin's methods. He had presumably fallen out of favor because of his objection to the first Moscow trial and was sent to the Caucasus in 1935 under outwardly honorable conditions. ("Remember, Abel," Stalin is reputed to have said, "who is not with me is against me.") Refusing to repent by pleading for Stalin's forgiveness, he was denied the presidency of the Transcaucasian Republic he had been originally offered and placed in charge of medical sanitoriums in Georgia. When he still refused to humble himself, Yagoda compiled an incriminating dossier, and the errant Yenukidze was expelled from the party for "political and moral dissoluteness." Warned that he would now have to confess his "crimes" publicly, he continued his stubborn silence, unconvinced that Stalin would pursue his feud to its logical conclusion. But treason and espionage charges inevitably followed, and Stalin's erstwhile "closest friend" was executed in December 1937.[8]

Once the sorcerer's apprentice of unrestrained terror gained momentum, Stalin found his economic and social goals in danger. The average factory worker or collective farmer was not apt to come under suspicion, but the attrition rate among the new technical intelligentsia was staggering. Although Stalin never openly repudiated his brutal tactics, he instituted a quiet purge of the purgers late in 1938. A fellow Georgian, Lavrenti Beria, replaced

Yezhov as chief of the N.K.V.D. in December, and the latter simply disappeared like so many of his victims. The circumstances were mysterious, but Yezhov is alleged to have brought about his own downfall by attempting to cast suspicion on Beria, then a potential rival. Beria requested Stalin to authorize an investigation, and Molotov headed a commission of inquiry that discovered dossiers on most of the members of the Politburo seeking to link them to subversive activities.[9] A high proportion of Yezhov's subordinates, down to the level of prison guards, shared his fate. Large scale arrests ceased, numerous sentences were suspended or curtailed, and conditions in the labor camps improved. But there was no general amnesty, and the police state that Stalin had molded to his will showed no signs of mellowing.

Indeed, Stalin continued to insist on summary punishment of his enemies but did not revert to the bloody holocaust of the 1930's. As the terror abated, a number of local party secretaries summoned the courage to protest the use of torture. But Stalin brusquely informed them in a coded telegram dispatched on January 20, 1939, that "physical pressure should still be used obligatorily, as an exception applicable to known and obstinate enemies of the people, as a method both justifiable and applicable." The vicious senselessness of his purge, though it had meaning and purpose in the context of Stalinism, has given rise to considerable speculation as to the dictator's sanity. Those who maintain that he was a paranoiac can cite Khrushchev in substantiation:

> Stalin was a very distrustful man, morbidly suspicious; we knew this from our work with him. He could look at a man and say: "Why are your eyes so shifty today?" or "Why are you turning so much today and why do you avoid looking directly into my eyes?" The sickly suspicion created in him a general distrust even toward eminent party workers whom he had known for years. Everywhere and in everything he saw "enemies," "two-facers" and "spies." [10]

If this testimony is trustworthy, one may certainly conclude that Stalin was mentally deranged. But we know from other sources—occasional interviews with foreigners and wartime meetings with diplomats and heads of state—that he spoke rationally and that his behavior was normal. The line between normal and abnormal is, of course, a thin one and more often a matter of "common sense" than a meaningful concept in psychiatry. The same can be said for "insanity," though it is a useful identifying label for one seriously divorced from reality. In this sense it is hardly possible to describe Stalin as insane, for his paranoid tendencies did not, as far as we know, incapacitate him for any length of time. His mental illness, such as it was, became progressively worse as he aged, and his final months were ridden with pathological fear and suspicion.

CHAPTER VII

The Comintern and International Politics

STALIN'S POLITICAL GIFTS WERE LESS IMPRESSIVE IN THE REALM OF diplomacy and foreign policy. If shrewd manipulation and naked coercion achieved the desired results on the domestic scene, such tactics were seldom appropriate in the international arena. Narrowly provincial in his intellectual horizons, he knew little of life outside the Soviet Union. Nor did he feel compelled to fill this yawning gap in his education, apparently content with the ready made formulas that Marxism supplied and supplemented by the superficial impressions acquired while on his trips abroad as a young revolutionary. Yet he was not without curiosity about foreign nations, and until the mid-thirties he received a number of "bourgeois" visitors from whom he usually solicited opinion and information about conditions in the capitalist countries.

As an aspirant to supreme power in the early twenties, Stalin was disinclined to interfere in the routine operations of the People's Commissariat for Foreign Affairs (Narkomindel) and took little interest, like most of the party elite, in diplomatic or commercial relations of the traditional sort. He shared, of course, in the policy formulations of the Politburo, which occasionally dealt with matters of diplomacy. Georgi Chicherin, the eccentric but gifted scholar-diplomat who presided over the destinies of the Narkomindel, came to dislike Stalin, and the feeling was mutual. In 1928 he was shunted aside in favor of his deputy, Maxim Litvinov, and was forced to retire two years later.

Stalin played a more active role in the affairs of the Communist International (Comintern), though Zinoviev's influence predominated until 1925. Following the fall of Bukharin in 1929 the Comintern was formally headed by a group of loyal Stalinists, of whom Molotov was the best known. The general secretary held a thoroughly cynical view of foreign Communism. "Who are these Comintern people?" he is said to have remarked at a Politburo meeting in 1927. "They are nothing but hirelings on our Soviet payroll. In ninety years they will never make a revolution anywhere."[1] But he was nevertheless careful not to abandon the theoretical goal of world Communism. Lacking the intellectual and emotional commitment of his colleagues, who were incapable of admitting that the militancy of the European proletariat was less a reality than an act of faith on their part, Stalin stood by his ideological stock-in-trade of "socialism in one country" and gave little more than lip service to the original Comintern aims. Under his supervision international Communism lost much of its revolutionary fervor and became an awkward and sometimes embarrassing appendage to the Kremlin's foreign policy.

Stalin's first important venture into the unfamiliar terrain of international politics ended in disaster—the Kuomintang-Communist alliance in China that collapsed in 1927. Perhaps in part because of this initial blunder, Stalin became excessively cautious about similar adventures abroad, and twenty years later he was still skeptical about the prospects of Chinese Communism. The original decision to send Soviet advisers to China and to provide material support to Sun Yat-sen's Kuomintang (National People's party) had been a collective one. It was fully in accord with Lenin's policy of collaboration with "bourgeois nationalist" groups to remove the shackles of capitalist imperialism in colonial and semi-colonial countries. The Kuomintang, somewhat precariously based in Canton, prepared to accept the fledgling Chinese Communist party as a junior partner in the effort to subdue the war lords and unify the nation.

Sun's death in 1925 elevated the ambitious young militarist Chiang Kai-shek to prominence as the leader of the Kuomintang's conservative faction. In 1926 Chiang's "northern expedition," which Stalin regarded as a foolhardy gamble, was more successful than the Kuomintang leaders had dared hope. It placed the Nationalist armies astride the Yangtze, and exactions upon the Shanghai business community relieved Chiang of humiliating financial dependence on Moscow. Hailed as a revolutionary hero by the world Communist press, he secretly prepared a "purification" campaign against his allies of the Communist party and the Kuomintang Left. Stalin convinced himself that Chiang was serving the Kremlin's ends: the Kuomintang Right would be "squeezed out like a lemon and then flung away," he told an audience of Moscow party workers on April 5, 1927.[2]

Stalin's complacency was rudely shattered a week later by Chiang's purge in Shanghai. Thousands of Communists, real and fancied, were slaughtered in a prolonged reign of terror that eventually enveloped the whole of Kuomintang China. Trotsky sought to capitalize on the debacle but was too weak politically even to gain a hearing in the press. Stalin blandly ignored the bankruptcy of his policy and compounded the original error by reaffirming the alliance with the Kuomintang Left, now established on the middle Yangtze in the tri-city area of Wuhan. "The bloody lesson of Shanghai passed without leaving a trace," Trotsky lamented from exile in 1930. "The Communists, as before, were being transformed into cattle herders for the party of the bourgeois executioners."

On June 1 Stalin directed the Comintern representatives in Wuhan to curb peasant "excesses" and to rid the Kuomintang of "unreliable generals," naive instructions that failed to grapple with the realities of power as the alliance disintegrated. The flower of the Wuhan army—much of it sympathetic to Communist aims—had recently perished in a bloody engagement with troops of the Manchurian war lord, and the peasant masses were the Kremlin's last hope of an ultimate Communist victory in China. As the leaders of the Kuomintang Left prepared to follow Chiang's lead with an anti-Communist purge, Stalin abruptly reversed himself. A Comintern pronouncement now exposed the Wuhan government as a "counter-revolutionary force" and denounced the Chinese Communist leaders for their "opportunist deviations." Mikhail Borodin, Moscow's chief agent, left China with other Soviet advisers, but Stalin decided to gamble on an adventurist policy. If collaboration and compromise had miscarried, then perhaps direct action would prevail. With the Chinese Communists properly chastised and new Soviet emissaries dispatched to the scene to insure compliance, a series of futile insurrections swept the countryside. In December 1927 these misguided tactics reached a new climax of *putschist* folly when several thousand Red Guards seized the city of Canton, only to be overwhelmed and massacred by Kuomintang troops. Stalin had timed the rising to coincide with the Fifteenth Party Congress in Moscow, where news of the anticipated victory would furnish a convincing display of his wisdom as the Trotskyist Opposition was drummed out of the party. It was far too late, however, for Trotsky to salvage his career with an exposé of his bungling rival.

The shattered remnants of the Chinese party retained a tenuous link with Moscow through the Comintern, but Stalin was illdisposed to meddle further in Chinese politics. Mao Tse-tung, the future leader of Red China, sought refuge with his small peasant army in the mountains of western Kiangsi. There, virtually autonomous and unencumbered by the fetish of Moscow's infallibility, his "Chinese Soviet Republic" grew strong enough within a few years to threaten the stability of the Kuomintang regime. If Stalin's opponents gained some political mileage from the abortive Chinese venture, their efforts to capitalize on Soviet setbacks in Europe were generally unavailing. In May 1927 the British government had severed diplomatic relations following a raid on the London quarters of the Soviet trade delegation, ostensibly in search of a missing War Office document. A concerted anti-Soviet campaign in France fell short of a similar rupture, but the Russian ambassador was declared *persona non grata* and obliged to leave. The Kremlin encouraged a war psychosis, already nurtured by years of propaganda about a "capitalist encirclement" and fresh memories of Allied intervention. Stalin saw that a war scare would further weaken the Opposition, for it was open to the charge of fostering disunity in party ranks while the nation faced the danger of foreign aggression. "Something like a united front from [British Foreign Secretary] Chamberlain to Trotsky is being formed," he quipped in a speech to the Comintern's executive committee.

During the late twenties foreign policy necessarily received a lower rating in the Kremlin's scale of priorities. Stalin was preoccupied with a variety of domestic crises, and the rise of fascism as an international menace was still in the future. Relations with Britain, while far from cordial, were normalized with an exchange of ambassadors in 1929. Germany remained Russia's only friend among the major powers, although time and circumstance had eroded the marriage of convenience consecrated by the Treaty of Rapallo in 1922. Germany was no longer a European pariah, and the shackles of the Versailles Treaty had been voluntarily loosened by the Entente powers. Rather than a formal estrangement, the two partners simply drifted apart.

The comparative serenity of European affairs did not extend to Asia. In 1929 the Soviet Union was embroiled in a minor war with China over the Chinese Eastern Railway, the Manchurian link between the Trans-Siberian Railroad and the Pacific port of Vladivostok. Manchurian troops, nominally under Chiang Kai-shek's authority, had seized the line in July and imprisoned Soviet nationals. In November, after negotiations failed, a small contingent of the Red Army occupied the railway zone against token resistance. Moscow's case was legally sound, but to many Communists the affair smacked of old fashioned imperialism. After all, Comintern propaganda had for years denounced the capitalist powers (including Tsarist Russia) for carving China into spheres of influence. Stalin scorned such arguments: his regime marked the transcendence of the Soviet national interest over the requirements of Communist ideology.

Even the "idealists" in the party acknowledged that if the Soviet government relinquished the railroad in an outburst of generosity, China was too weak to hold it should Japan resume an expansionist policy on the Asiatic mainland. Less than two years later the Japanese militarists, kept in check for almost a decade, launched an invasion of Manchuria. The great powers intervened with ringing salvoes of moral indignation and an investigation by the League of Nations. The Soviet Union derided the hypocrisy of the League's Commission of Inquiry but refused to cooperate with its efforts and demonstrated as much reluctance as the Western nations to become involved in a shooting war. Without a hint of alarm in the press, the country underwent a war scare as genuine as that of 1927 had been contrived. In 1933 Moscow sought to rid itself of the strategically untenable Manchurian railway by selling it to Manchukuo—the Japanese puppet state. After a two year delay and intermittent bargaining the line was sold for less than $40,000,000, a fraction of the original construction cost.

Obviously worried about Japan's future intentions, the Kremlin made discreet overtures to Washington regarding possible diplomatic collaboration. Such proposals were futile, for the United States did not contemplate flouting the overwhelmingly isolationist sentiment of its people. One concession was granted by the new administration of President Franklin D. Roosevelt in 1933: official recognition of the Soviet Union after a sixteen year diplomatic boycott. But predictions that the two governments might find common ground in "quarantining" the aggressor were disappointed. Washington displayed no disposition to surmount the petty annoyances that plagued its relations with Moscow and consistently took a legalistic view of the difficulties.

Although the revival of Japanese imperialism was a serious threat to Soviet interests, the rise of Nazi Germany dwarfed the potential danger from the east. Stalin, like the politicians of democratic countries, was slow to grasp the latent dynamism of German-style fascism. Communist theoreticians had been content to label the phenomenon of fascism—heretofore known chiefly as an Italian product—as the decadent stage of monopoly capitalism. German Communists, in obedience to the Comintern's dictates, had attacked their Social Democratic rivals as "social fascists" who were betraying the working class. The National Socialists (Nazis) were merely the pathological but harmless grave diggers of capitalism. Even with Adolf Hitler and his Nazi henchmen in power in 1933, the Comintern leaders in Moscow solemnly intoned the Stalinist catechism: "The conquest of power by Hitler does not signify a defeat for the Communist Party and the working class. The revolutionary upsurge has been temporarily interrupted." [3]

Stalin offered no fundamental reassessment of his German policy until 1934. Meanwhile, Moscow prepared to do business in the Rapallo tradition and to ignore the fate of its German confreres. "We are far from being enthusiastic about the fascist regime in Germany," Stalin announced. "But it is not a question of fascism here, if only for the reason that fascism in Italy, for example, has not prevented the U.S.S.R. from establishing the best relations with that country." But the Nazi regime, drugged on the ideology of anti-Communism, made it clear that German-Soviet friendship was at an end. As the German ambassador to Moscow put it in his final report before being transferred to Tokyo in August 1933: "The Rapallo chapter is closed."

Having proceeded on the assumption that all bourgeois governments were fundamentally alike, the Kremlin was forced to discard a number of acquired prejudices. The old predators of capitalism—Britain, France, and the United States—seemed toothless indeed beside Nazi Germany and Imperial Japan. The Versailles Treaty was no longer considered so iniquitous an example of Allied imperialism, and the League of Nations lost its status as an "alliance of world bandits" (Lenin's phrase). In December 1933 Stalin foreshadowed his own "agonizing reappraisal" by declaring that "notwithstanding its colossal defects" Soviet support for the League was "not impossible." A month later at the Seventeenth Party Congress he warned the aggressor nations: "Those who want peace and seek business relations with us will always have our support. But those who try to attack our country will receive a stunning rebuff to teach them not to poke their pig's snout into our Soviet garden again."

By 1934 a rapprochement with France was well under way, and in September of that year Moscow joined the League of Nations. Litvinov presided over the new policy of "collective security," and though he symbolized to most Westerners Soviet leadership in the struggle against international fascism in the 1930's, his authority never exceeded the limited autonomy that was Stalin's privilege to revoke at any time. The principal edifice of Russia's new security system in Europe was a defensive alliance with France signed in May 1935. A similar pact with Czechoslovakia was arranged shortly afterward. For a variety of reasons, chiefly French reluctance to implement the pact with appropriate military and diplomatic measures, the Franco-Soviet treaty remained a paper commitment that did little more than irritate Nazi Germany.

A belated reversal of the obsolete Comintern line was formally authorized at the Seventh World Congress in Moscow during the summer of 1935. The French Communists, mindful of the German lesson, had already pioneered an anti-fascist coalition with the Socialists and Radicals. Stalin hand-picked their party chieftain, Maurice Thorez, and summoned him to Moscow in the spring of 1934 to receive the new dispensation. France therefore became the model for a world-wide "popular front" against fascism. The baptismal rites were performed in Paris on July 14, 1935—Bastille Day—at a monster demonstration in which the tricolor and the red flag flew side by side while the "International" and the "Marseillaise" vied for vocal support. As a tactical spinoff of Moscow's strategy of collective security, the Popular Front movement had some fleeting but tangible success in France, Spain, and China. A significant by-product was the acceptance of Communism as a respectable cause in the democratic West, not for its intrinsic merit but because of its courageous stand against fascism. To many intellectuals not otherwise attracted by political panaceas, Stalin's Russia seemed imbued with virtues that their own pusillanimous governments lacked. To Stalin himself the struggle against fascism was not a question of principle but one of expediency—of protecting the national interest by whatever methods seemed appropriate at the time.

The course of the Spanish Civil War provided a microcosm of World War II and a test case for collective security. The conflict began in July 1936 when an ultra-conservative military clique rose against the Popular Front government. General Francisco Franco, shortly to be invested with the leadership of the Nationalist rebels, represented the Falange movement—the Spanish equivalent of Italy's Fascist party. Lacking the demagogic mystique of a Hitler or Mussolini, he strove conscientiously to bolster the junta's meager popular appeal with the trite phrases of pseudo-radicalism. An improvised workers' militia upset the Nationalist timetable, and in the fall the arrival of Soviet war matériel and noncombatant specialists partially offset the growing army of German and Italian "volunteers." On the strength of Moscow's limited assistance—and the service rendered by the Comintern in recruiting the International Brigades—the Spanish

Communist party flourished in numbers and prestige. It became a relatively moderate element in the government coalition, and the Socialist gibe, "Vote Communist to save Spain from Marxism," was an apt commentary on the non-revolutionary role of international Communism during the heyday of the Popular Front.

To insure rigid obedience to the Kremlin line, Stalin dispatched his own agents to supplement—or to displace—the indigenous Communist leadership. The methods of the Soviet secret police were exported to Spain with them, and in the guise of liquidating "Trotskyism" many dissident Leftists were ruthlessly purged by extra-legal means. Whether by coincidence or design, an abnormally large proportion of Russians who served in Spain were arrested or executed upon their return. Probably Stalin considered them tainted by political or ideological impurities acquired abroad. His distrust of foreign Communists, especially those suspected of unorthodox views, was notorious. Hundreds who sought refuge in the Soviet Union from political persecution disappeared during the Great Purge.

The Western powers pursued the farce of non-intervention, refusing even to sell arms to the Spanish Republic. Discouraged by the attitude of their prospective allies and preoccupied with other diplomatic concerns, the Russians curtailed their aid in 1937, and it ceased altogether in the summer of 1938. The fate of Spanish democracy—Franco's victorious troops entered Madrid in March 1939—furnished a muted anti-climax to Hitler's peaceful conquest of Central Europe. Austria had been absorbed by the German Reich in March 1938, placing Czechoslovakia squarely in the path of the Nazi juggernaut. The British and French governments studiously ignored the Soviet Union throughout the ensuing crisis over the Sudetenland—the strategic Czech border territory that Hitler claimed because of its German population. Moscow repeatedly assured the Czechs that it would carry out its treaty obligations. Whether the pledge was sincere, and if so whether effective assistance could be rendered through neutral Poland or Romania, was never put to the test. Prague capitulated on September 30 as Britain and France accepted the German demands at the Munich Conference. Nazi troops poured into the remainder of Czechoslovakia the following March.

The Kremlin's unrewarding courtship of the Western powers reached its nadir with the Munich Pact. As a Soviet diplomat remarked to the French ambassador to Moscow shortly afterward: "My poor friend, what have you done? For us I see no other way out than a fourth partition of Poland." [4] Unable to comprehend the longing for peace and the failure of nerve that had led to such abject humiliation, Stalin suspected treachery. He became convinced that Hitler was being offered a blank check in the East. Such thoughts did not come as a sudden revelation, for the Soviet dictator was a hardened practitioner of *Realpolitik* and had not chosen to collaborate with Britain and France through motives of idealism. If the Nazi leaders had been less intoxicated by their propaganda about an "international Jewish-Marxist conspiracy" emanating from Moscow they might have listened to his cautious feelers in the winter of 1936–1937.

Soviet policy changed subtly and gradually. In October 1938 Litvinov reached an oral agreement with the German ambassador to moderate the intemperate radio and press exchange between the two countries. In November an address by Molotov departed from the conventional tone of anti-fascist rhetoric by warning of a "second imperialist war [which] has already begun on an immense field from Gibraltar to Shanghai." In December the two powers signed a routine trade agreement without the usual delays attending such transactions. At a diplomatic reception in January 1939 Hitler spoke longer to the Soviet ambassador than to anyone else. But not until the Eighteenth Party Congress in March did Stalin convey a veiled invitation to Berlin. His remarks, while still couched in the idiom of collective security, referred to the coming "imperialist struggle" in terms of vintage Marxism. His analysis of Anglo-French appeasement was bitterly sarcastic, and he warned the party "to be cautious and not allow one country to be drawn into conflicts by warmongers who are accustomed to have others pull the chestnuts out of the fire for them." He reminded those "case-hardened bourgeois diplomats" that Russia too could be perfidious: "The big and dangerous political game started by the supporters of nonintervention [i.e., appeasement] may end in a serious fiasco for them." On the other hand, if there really were "lunatics in Germany" with designs on the Soviet Ukraine, "rest assured that we shall find enough straitjackets for them."

Stalin had not yet burned his bridges with the West. He seemed content to bide his time and await the best offer. But on May 3, after London and Paris had rejected a Soviet proposal for a binding military alliance, he indicated his preference for an accommodation with Berlin by accepting Litvinov's "resignation" and appointing Molotov as a replacement. As a Jew and the showpiece of collective security, Litvinov was an obvious sacrificial offering prior to serious negotiations with the Nazis. Under

Molotov the Narkomindel completed its transformation from a relatively cosmopolitan haven for Old Bolsheviks to a bureaucratic instrument of Stalin's will.

Hitler was now interested in a political understanding with Moscow in preparation for his forthcoming assault on Poland. With no scruples about partitioning eastern Europe, he could easily outbid Britain and France. Had the negotiations been left to the Nazi leadership, an agreement might never have been reached. So deep-rooted was their antagonism that neither power quite believed that the other was not using it as a pawn for diplomatic trickery. The German embassy in Moscow, however, was staffed with professionals in the Bismarckian tradition, and in July the protracted commercial talks at last verged on politics. In mid-August, when Moscow was assured of Germany's seriousness, Molotov raised the possibility of a non-aggression pact. The Nazi foreign minister, Joachim von Ribbentrop, replied favorably and offered to fly to Moscow to work out the details. Stalin still procrastinated, but when a commercial treaty was signed in Berlin on August 19 and Hitler himself sent a personal message urging immediate action, he consented to receive Ribbentrop.

The German delegation arrived on the 23rd and remained closeted with Stalin and Molotov, with a lengthy dinner recess, until a treaty of friendship and non-aggression was signed in the early morning of the 24th. In a secret protocol partitioning eastern Europe into spheres of influence, the Soviet portion included Finland, Latvia, Estonia, eastern Poland, and Bessarabia. Although Germany disclaimed interest in southeastern Europe, the failure to deal more explicitly with the Balkans was a source of future trouble. Stalin considered his handiwork a diplomatic triumph—and so it seemed at the time. He had secured for his country a spectator's role in the impending European conflict and gained precious time to push ahead with the third Five Year Plan and various measures of military preparedness. He also acquired a buffer zone that breached the anti-Soviet *cordon sanitaire* of 1919 and offered protection against Nazi duplicity. He could not foresee—nor did any Western politician—the crushing military power of Nazi Germany. A champagne party completed the night's work. Stalin, apparently projecting his own idealized relationship with the Russian people, offered a toast to Hitler: "I know how much the German nation loves its Führer." [5]

In retrospect the Nazi-Soviet Pact followed logically from Moscow's disillusionment with collective security. Yet news of the volte-face astonished the presumably well informed as much as it did the general public. The Anglo-French delegation in the Soviet capital, hopeful of an anti-Nazi alliance with the Russians, was caught flatfooted. The crushing blow to international Communism and the ideology of the Popular Front left Stalin unmoved. Not equally impervious to internal public opinion, he objected to Ribbentrop's bombastic draft communiqué: "For many years now we have been pouring buckets of slop over each other's heads, and our propaganda boys could never do enough in that direction; and now all of a sudden are we to make our peoples believe that all is forgotten and forgiven?" [6] His suggestion of a more straightforward announcement was readily accepted.

None of the powers was more shocked and indignant than Germany's Axis partner, Japan. A series of Soviet-Japanese border clashes—heavy fighting was then under way near Lake Buir on the Mongolian-Manchurian frontier—convinced Tokyo that the rich colonial empires of Britain, France, and the Netherlands offered easier plunder than Outer Mongolia and the Soviet Far East. Japan remained aloof from the European war and concentrated on winding up the "China affair." The Tokyo militarists had invaded China proper following the Marco Polo Bridge incident in July 1937, but a decisive victory continued to elude them. Until Russia was itself attacked in 1941, Soviet military aid and technical advice became one of the mainstays of Chinese resistance. Supplies were funneled exclusively to the Nationalist government. The Kremlin officially ignored the Communists, whose uneasy collaboration with Chiang against the Japanese hardly amounted to more than an armed truce after 1940.

Poland's swift collapse before the Nazi onslaught caught Stalin by surprise. He was obliged to move rapidly to collect the Polish spoils promised in the secret protocol, and the Red Army began occupying its assigned sphere on September 17. A subsequent agreement with Germany reduced the Soviet share to a more ethnically justifiable frontier. In return, Hitler conceded most of Lithuania to the Russian sphere. Moscow absorbed the three Baltic republics as military protectorates, preserving their autonomy for the time being.

Finland proved more resistant to Soviet pressure tactics. Leningrad lay within artillery range of the Finnish frontier, and the city was exposed to an attack through the Gulf of Finland. Stalin took personal charge of the negotiations. His demands—chiefly a boundary adjustment, a demilitarized border, and naval bases in the Gulf of Finland—were not unreasonable in the context of great power politics. Yet Helsinki's case was morally and legally impregnable, and the Finns had grown too accustomed to Russia's exemplary conduct during the previous twenty years to expect a solution by military force. The terms were partially rejected and the discussions broken off.

On November 30, 1939, after Moscow had contrived a border incident, the Red Army was set in motion. Its initial performance was so inept that Western military experts concluded almost to a man that the purges had eliminated the Soviet Union as a first rate military power for the foreseeable future. Stalin had deluded himself that the war could be won with a few inferior divisions, for it seemed obvious that the Finnish masses would refuse to rally behind their "reactionary" government. The gallant stand of little Finland won the astonished admiration of world opinion, and Anglo-French military strategists, unwilling to carry the fight to Germany, concocted a harebrained scheme to strike at the Soviet Union through the Scandinavian countries and the Middle East. The League of Nations, moribund after years of placating the Axis powers, was abruptly resurrected to chastise the Russians. Moscow was solemnly expelled in mid-December with an appropriate resolution of censure. The action could only have strengthened Stalin's conviction that Western appeasement had been a calculated attempt to turn the German menace eastward.

Confronted with an embarrassing and potentially dangerous situation, the Soviet Union began a well prepared frontal offensive on February 1, 1940, that forced the Finns to submit. The peace terms, while harsher than those offered in October, were more generous than Moscow could have exacted and did not impair Finnish independence. Helsinki was outraged by the settlement, however, and drifted toward a pro-German policy that was to compound the original tragedy.

The fate of Finland, which had loomed so large in world affairs during the winter, was all but forgotten in the spring as the Wehrmacht overwhelmed Denmark, Norway, Holland, Belgium, and France in swift succession. The Kremlin had anticipated a war of attrition on the western front not unlike that of 1914–1918, and its alarm at sharing the European continent with such a powerful "friend" was barely concealed. The failure of *Pravda* and *Izvestia* to publish a lead article or editorial on the war during the month of June was in itself eloquent testimony to Stalin's dismay. The three Baltic republics, whose "independence" was subject to abrogation at any moment, were annexed as constituent parts of the U.S.S.R. in August. Bessarabia, lost to Romania in 1918, was reannexed at the same time. Moscow was in no position to acknowledge the strategic rationale of the move, nor was it seemly to refer to the Tsarist title deeds to furnish a legal gloss to the transaction.

Stalin also had designs on the Romanian province of Bukovina, whose large Ukrainian minority provided an excuse for intervention. Berlin's attitude was so inscrutable that Moscow settled for the northern portion. Hitler secretly advised Bucharest that the Soviet occupation was only a "temporary adjustment" to be rectified in due course. Thereafter German-Soviet relations deteriorated from a state of surface cordiality to one of strained politeness. Already, by the late summer of 1940, Hitler had decided in principle that an invasion of the Soviet Union would be launched in the spring. The decision was a personal one, and though presumably subject to revision it could not be influenced by Moscow's behavior—whether fawning or truculent. Although the evidence of Germany's intentions began to accumulate over a period of months, Stalin convinced himself that adroit diplomacy and a "correct" attitude would ward off the Nazi danger.

If a chance for peace remained, the opportunity passed in November 1940 when Molotov went to Berlin for a briefing on Hitler's grandiose project of global partition. Moscow was promised a sphere of influence in the Middle East, not an uninviting prospect had Berlin also been willing to leave the Russians a clear field in the Balkans. Stalin's formal answer to the proposed treaty between the Soviet Union and the three Axis powers was favorable but qualified. He made no blanket demands for a Balkan preserve—Romania was already a German satellite—but asked that Bulgaria and the Turkish Straits be included in the Soviet "security zone." Finland, already invested with German troops, was to be restored to its previous status. Hitler concluded that Moscow was unwilling to concede eastern Europe—in other words, that Soviet foreign policy would remain independent and therefore a potential threat to the security of the greater Reich. He refused even the courtesy of a reply and in December sent a memorandum to his commanders proposing to "crush Soviet Russia in a quick campaign." The target date was May 15, 1941.

Moscow recorded only one diplomatic victory in the year preceding the German attack—a neutrality pact with Japan. As the Japanese drive into South Asia and the Pacific gained momentum in 1940–1941, the necessity of safeguarding their rear from the

Soviet Union became more pressing. Tokyo failed to interest the Kremlin in a non-aggression pact on the Soviet-German model, and a simple treaty of neutrality was signed on April 13, 1941, after negotiations in Moscow between Stalin and Yosuke Matsuoka, the Japanese foreign minister. A mutually beneficial arrangement, it proved of greater advantage to the Russians in the long run. Berlin had previously urged such an agreement on its Oriental partner. Hitler was so confident of success in Russia that he valued Japan more as an ally against Britain and a barrier to American intervention in the European war than as a co-belligerent against the Soviet Union. Stalin capped the Matsuoka visit with an unprecedented appearance at the railway station to bid his guest farewell. He not only embraced Matsuoka but startled the attending German ambassador and the military attaché with vigorous hugs and an expressed wish for friendly relations. The scene was staged to impress Hitler with his sincere desire for peace.

At the time of Stalin's well publicized performance at the railway station the Nazi legions were once again demonstrating their mechanized prowess. Yugoslavia and Greece, the last neutral states in eastern Europe, were the victims. The price of victory was to prove costly—a five week postponement of the Russian campaign. Stalin strove mightily to convince the Germans that he had lost interest in the Balkans. Aside from minor gestures of propitiation, he took over from Molotov on May 6 the chairmanship of the Council of People's Commissars—the premiership. It was his first government office since relinquishing the post of commissar for nationalities over two decades before. Having legalized his status as the Soviet ruler, he demonstrated his readiness to accept whatever new proposals Hitler might offer. Berlin maintained an eloquent silence. The Kremlin made an attempt to draw out the Germans on June 13 when the Soviet press accused the British ambassador of instigating "absurd" rumors about the "proximity of war between the Soviet Union and Germany" and credited the Nazis with "strictly observing" the non-aggression pact.

Again there was no reaction from Berlin—not even a news item in the press. Puzzled, the Kremlin authorized its ambassador in Berlin to make discreet inquiries about Germany's attitude. He could get no satisfactory answer. Ribbentrop, for example, was "out of town." On June 21 Molotov summoned the German ambassador, Werner von der Schulenburg, to his office and taxed him about the increasing number of border violations by German aircraft. He appeared genuinely bewildered by the deterioration of German-Soviet relations and asked almost plaintively if Schulenburg "could tell him what had brought about the present situation." Embarrassed, the ambassador declined comment—he "lacked the pertinent information"—and gave the routine reply that he would pass on Molotov's remarks to his superiors.[7]

At 4 A.M. the following morning Schulenburg entered the Kremlin for the last time. His mission was to deliver a statement by Ribbentrop justifying Germany's action in violating the treaty of friendship and non-aggression. Communist Russia and Nazi Germany were at war.

CHAPTER VIII

The War Leader

GERMAN FORCES CROSSED THE RUSSIAN FRONTIER IN THE EARLY morning of June 22, 1941. They achieved virtually complete tactical surprise despite repeated warnings from British, American, and Soviet intelligence sources that an attack was imminent. Stalin had convinced himself that Hitler would not move against him—at least not for some months—and dismissed the reports as lies and provocations. Unlimited power and excessive adulation had blunted his judgment. Events forced him to admit his fallibility, a rare moment of self-analysis that apparently so unnerved him that he remained in seclusion for almost two weeks. The task of informing the public was left to Molotov, who made a nationwide broadcast several hours after the Nazi invasion.

The initial German onslaught succeeded beyond all expectation. Most of the Soviet air force was destroyed on the ground, and an over-concentration of men and equipment near the border area led to a debacle that seemed to confirm Hitler's boast: "We have only to kick in the door and the whole rotten structure will come crashing down." If Khrushchev is to be believed, Stalin was ready to concede that all had been lost. His "nervousness and hysteria" interfered with military operations and caused "serious damage" to the Red Army.

Stalin awoke from his mood of fatalistic lethargy on July 3 when he addressed the nation by radio. Although his voice was slow and monotonous, and his speech colorless and rather pedantic, the total effect was impressive. His opening words struck a humble note that was extraordinary in itself: "Comrades, citizens, brothers and sisters, men of our Army and Navy! My words are addressed to you, dear friends!" (As a former Soviet official remarked, "The Boss must have been in a pretty bad way to call us brothers and sisters.") [1] He admitted the gravity of the situation while deliberately concealing the extent of the German breakthrough, falsely claiming that "the enemy's finest divisions and finest air force units have already been smashed." He went on to justify his pact with Germany despite its leadership by

"such perfidious people, such fiends as Hitler and Ribbentrop."
He then came to the substance of his message—the "patriotic war
of liberation against the fascist enslavers." After conventional ex-
hortations to defend the fatherland and to eliminate cowards, de-
serters, panic-mongers, spies, and diversionists, he made a ringing
plea for "scorched earth" tactics: "The enemy must not be left a
single engine, a single railway car, not a single pound of grain or
gallon of fuel." Guerrilla units and saboteurs must "blow up
bridges and roads, damage telephone and telegraph lines, set fire
to forests, stores and transports." In occupied areas the enemy
"must be hounded and annihilated at every step." The people
should "rally around the Party of Lenin and Stalin. . . . Forward to victory!" [2]

The address restored Stalin's moral authority and furnished
the image if not the reality of the wise and powerful leader who
would vanquish the enemy and drive him from the homeland. If
he had not existed, it would have been necessary to create him.
Like Winston Churchill and Franklin D. Roosevelt, he embodied
in the popular mind the heroism and sacrifice of the national war
effort. He lacked the personality and eloquence of the two democratic rulers, but his brooding presence in the Kremlin offered
solid reassurance that the Russian state still endured.

During the dictator's lifetime the legend of the heroic war
leader was carried to fatuous extremes. Not content with the servile flattery that proclaimed his talents as a statesman and ideologue—the "genius-leader and teacher of all progressive mankind" in *Pravda*'s unctuous phrase—he also posed as a master of
military strategy. Beginning in 1943 every triumph of the Red
Army was hailed as further evidence of his unique gifts. Even his
mistakes—and he was to admit in 1945 that mistakes had been
made—were eventually transmuted into farsighted wisdom. The
headlong Soviet retreat in 1941 was acclaimed a masterpiece of
military planning in which the Germans had been lured into the
depths of the country to insure their future annihilation.

In 1956 Khrushchev's anti-Stalinist outburst included a deadly
thrust at the supreme commander's reputation. The *Vozhd* was
portrayed as a stubborn bungler who ignored sound advice and
in late 1941 ordered "incessant frontal attacks" until his generals
were able to salvage the situation with more flexible tactics. We
are also told that he planned his military operations on a globe,
an allegation that strains credulity because of his civil war experience and the recollection of various Allied officials that he had
an excellent grasp of military problems.

What, then, was Stalin's true role as supreme commander? Certainly it was far less significant than his propagandists tried to convey, yet it seems to have been of more positive substance than Khrushchev's derogatory verdict leads one to suppose. He was essentially a coordinator whose chief contribution lay in the administration of the total war effort rather than supervising specific campaigns. As a battlefield tactician he was strictly an amateur, and his ventures in that direction were often disastrous. But he was a shrewd judge of military as well as civilian skills, and the generals who emerged under his leadership were among the most talented in modern history.

Stalin's wartime powers rested—legally speaking—upon a formidable array of titles and official functions. He had already completed the fusion of party and government with his assumption of the premiership. On June 30 he became chairman of the newly established State Committee for Defense, a kind of special war cabinet whose roster included Molotov, Voroshilov, Beria, and Georgi Malenkov. He was also a member of *Stavka*—the supreme military command—and on July 19 he added the Commissariat of Defense to his growing list of offices. On August 7 he officially became commander-in-chief of the armed forces, and in March 1943 he assumed the rank of marshal. Generalissimo, an honorific title conferred in 1945, was specially created to celebrate the triumph over Germany.

In the summer of 1941 the front was divided into three sectors: the northern under Voroshilov, the southern under Budyonny, and the central under Semyon Timoshenko. The first two choices reflected Stalin's preference for commanders whose personal loyalty was unquestioned. But they quickly demonstrated incompetence in mechanized warfare, and Stalin dismissed them in the fall as the Wehrmacht routed a Russian army of a million men near Kiev and threatened Moscow and Leningrad. His own conception of proper tactics—that of static defense—was faulty, and his order to "Stand fast, hold out, and if need be die" was probably more to blame for the Soviet defeat at Kiev than Budyonny's inept generalship. Timoshenko performed more capably, although his reputation was eventually overshadowed by a brilliant group of younger officers headed by Georgi Zhukov. Stalin had some of his generals shot for their failure to halt the Germans in the first months of the war. On the other hand, he rehabilitated many victims of his military purge; some officers were abruptly transferred from prison and labor camps to combat assignments.

In his contacts with Allied officials during the summer and fall of 1941, Stalin was imperturbable and confident of ultimate victory. Privately, however, he must have had moments of doubt, if not something akin to panic. The Red Army had not become a disorganized rabble, but a former Soviet general has bluntly stated that it was a "hopeless mess" from the second day of the war.[3] A measure of Stalin's desperation is revealed by his offer to Harry L. Hopkins, President Roosevelt's special representative, to allow American troops to fight under their own commanders on any part of the Russian front. The British were also invited to send troops to the Ukrainian front. Neither Washington nor London seriously considered the possibility, and Stalin did not renew his overtures. As the Germans approached Moscow in late autumn, he displayed some apprehension to the British ambassador. Conceding that the Soviet capital might be taken, he nevertheless maintained that the Red Army would continue the fight even if forced to retreat beyond the Volga.

On November 7 Stalin reviewed his troops from the Lenin mausoleum in Red Square, an annual custom on the revolutionary holiday. His speech, a rousing patriotic appeal, evoked the heroes of Russia's past: "The war you are fighting is a war of liberation, a just war. May you be inspired . . . by the heroic examples of our great ancestors—Alexander Nevsky, Dmitri Donskoi, Kuzma Minin, Dmitri Pozharsky, Alexander Suvorov, Mikhail Kutuzov! May the victorious banner of the great Lenin embrace you! . . . Death to the German invaders! Long live our glorious country, its freedom, its independence! Under the banner of Lenin—forward to victory!" [4] After the ceremonies most of the detachments marched directly to defensive positions in the suburbs. Most government offices, the embassies, and many factories had already been evacuated, and thousands of panicky civilians fled the apparently doomed city. Stalin chose to remain in the Kremlin, an example of fortitude that helped raise the morale of the besieged and furnished a symbol of resistance for the country as a whole. As Georgi Dimitrov, the Bulgarian Communist leader, testified: "One cannot express how great a moral significance was exerted when people learned that Stalin was sitting in the Kremlin. . . . It restored their faith and raised their confidence, and it was worth more than a good-sized army." [5]

Zhukov commanded the Russian armies before Moscow as the Germans launched their final assault in mid-November. The muddy roads that had slowed the advance were now firm under a heavy frost. But as the weather turned colder the Wehrmacht was crippled by lack of winter equipment, most obviously the warm clothing that was standard in the Red Army. Frostbite became the Russians' best ally. With the outskirts of the city almost in sight, the Nazi offensive spent itself during the first week in December. The Germans tried in vain to dig in for the winter as Zhukov mounted a counterattack that pushed the front back 150 miles in most sectors. Crack units from eastern Siberia—the Kremlin's intelligence network reported that Japan's Manchurian army would not strike—furnished a manpower reserve that Hitler could not match.

With the coming of spring Stalin faced the renewed campaign with confidence, perhaps overconfidence, since he launched the premature slogan "Victory in 1942." He may have believed it possible to defeat the Germans within the next few months, but it seems more likely that he sought to encourage the population with a deliberately optimistic rallying cry. The United States was now an ally, and the supplies promised the previous year under the Lend-Lease program began to arrive in more than token quantity. Russians, however, not British and Americans, sustained the war against Nazi Germany. As Soviet casualties mounted during the summer of 1942 and his allies offered no hope of a major diversionary effort, Stalin began to suspect that a mutual bloodletting was part of the Anglo-American strategy. Molotov, after a mission to London and Washington in the late spring, had returned with a promise of action before the end of the year. The British had reservations, but Stalin regarded the ambiguous understanding as a firm commitment for a landing in France. He was therefore outraged when in August Churchill flew to Moscow and told him bluntly that an invasion of Europe would not be attempted that year. Bitterly disappointed, he was almost insulting as he implied that the Western powers were afraid to meet the Germans on the battlefield. He was mollified to some extent when informed of the Anglo-American assault on French North Africa planned for October. His comment, "May God prosper this undertaking," was the disconcerting benediction of an avowed atheist.

Russia's military postion, less precarious than in 1941, still hovered on the edge of disaster. Hitler had abandoned the drive on Moscow to strike at the lower Don region and the oil of the Caucasus. Defense in depth and tactical withdrawals could have blunted the German assault. Stalin thought otherwise, having failed to absorb the lessons of 1941. His elite units, well equipped with heavy tanks, were dispersed in three separate attacks: the

Crimean Peninsula, the Volkhov River near Leningrad, and Kharkov in the Ukraine. Each thrust was shattered in turn, a triple fiasco that eased the path of the German *Blitzkrieg* as it rolled across the open plains of southern Russia. Rostov, on the lower Don, fell in late July, and Stalingrad, originally a second-ary objective on the Volga, lay exposed to the enemy.

For reasons of prestige as well as strategy, "Stalin's city" became a focal point for both armies. "Not another step backward," Sta-lin ordered on September 7. "The Volga has now only one bank." He placed Zhukov, the savior of Moscow, in supreme command and dispatched Nikita Khrushchev to the scene as his political representative. By late October the Germans had cut the city in half and reached the Volga. Meanwhile Russian reserves were brought up for a vast encircling operation designed to crush the enemy between converging spearheads. The plans had been worked out in the Kremlin under Stalin's supervision, though his tactical contribution was probably meager. The counter-offensive began on November 19. Within four days the trap was shut, but the Germans might have broken out with a fighting retreat had not Hitler ordered his commanders to hold fast. The Russians gradually constricted the ring, and in early February 1943 the beaten remnants of the German Sixth Army—some 91,000 officers and men—surrendered. The battle of Stalingrad, the savage cli-max to the Russo-German conflict (and to World War II) shat-tered Hitler's dream of conquering the Soviet Union. Never again did the Wehrmacht mount a sustained offensive on any front.

Russia did not win the war at Stalingrad. More than two years of hard fighting lay ahead. But the fatherland had survived the worst—and with it Stalin's regime. Thousands of Soviet citizens, especially the national minorities in the border areas, had been prepared to meet the Germans as liberators. Some did become collaborators; most, however, were quickly disabused of their il-lusions by the calculated brutality of German occupation policy. The invaders came as conquerors, not as emancipators of op-pressed nationalities—or even as fascist proseletizers solicitous to save the population from "Jewish Bolshevism." Nazi racial theory numbered Slavs among the *Untermenschen*—subhumans—and this contempt for the Russian people inevitably rubbed off on the German soldier. The shooting of hostages, the destruction of cul-tural shrines, the starvation of war prisoners, the drafting of forced labor for German war industries, the extermination of Soviet Jews—this was standard operating procedure, not the sadistic whim of a few military commanders or occupation authorities. Stalin's onetime distinction between the German people and their Nazi masters was forgotten until the closing stages of the war. He himself invariably concluded his orders of the day with the refrain, "Death to the German invaders!"

Like Hitler, but for different reasons, Stalin avoided a conflict of ideologies. He did not abandon Communism; rather did he place his doctrinal system in suspended animation for the duration. His rhetoric was that of Russian nationalism, for he recognized that the masses would not respond to the catch phrases of Marxism or to the clichés of Stalinism. The political reliability of the Red Army was in some doubt during the early stages of the war, and special units of the N.K.V.D. were on hand to check panic and prevent unauthorized retreat. As Stalin remarked cryptically in reply to the American ambassador's praise for the bravery of Russian troops in a particular engagement, "In the Soviet Army it takes more courage to retreat than to advance." [6] Despite indications of shaky morale in the summer of 1941, the courage and fighting quality of the common soldier was the vital ingredient of ultimate victory. Guerrilla bands, fighting in the German rear, supplemented regular units and exemplified the grim determination of the ordinary citizen to expel the hated invader. Gradually, as the performance of his troops reassured Stalin and no major signs of disaffection appeared among his officers, he sanctioned a return to military professionalism. The revolutionary heritage of the Red Army all but vanished during the war. Political commissars—in effect, dual military command—were abolished in 1942, and a host of measures strengthened the status and prestige of the officer corps. The return to tradition was completed in 1946 when the Red Army lost its colorful identity and became simply the Soviet Army.

The concessions granted the Orthodox Church furnished a more striking example of Stalin's retreat from Bolshevik dogma. Atheism was an immutable principle of Soviet ideology, and the government's policy toward organized religion had vacillated between severe persecution and reluctant toleration. The cruder varieties of anti-religious propaganda had been muted in the late thirties. The chief "godless" journal, a weekly published by the League of Militant Atheists, was suspended shortly after the war began because of the "paper shortage." In September 1943 a de facto concordat between church and state was arranged following Stalin's meeting in the Kremlin with leading ecclesiastical officials. The church was allowed to elect a patriarch, to govern its own affairs through a Holy Synod, to open a number of seminaries, and to own property. In return for these and other favors, the church gave vigorous support to the war effort and conferred its blessing upon the Soviet regime, including Stalin himself as head of state. The arrangement was mutually beneficial and so politically motivated that Stalin's attitude toward religion could hardly have been involved. Yet there was talk in Moscow that he had a soft spot for the church, presumably because of his seminary background. He did consider it politic to profess a certain religiosity, at least to foreigners, for he told the British ambassador that "in his own way, he also believed in God." [7]

Wartime expediency was not confined to domestic institutions. The Marxist theory that wars are rooted in the economic rivalry of capitalist powers was temporarily discarded and a sharp distinction drawn between democratic and fascist states. As symbolic reassurance that the regime had repudiated the doctrine of the class struggle, the "International," that rousing hymn to proletarian militancy, was replaced as the Soviet national anthem by a conventional homily to Russian patriotism. And as a token of good will toward his allies, Stalin formally abolished the Comintern in May 1943. "The Westerners are so sly that they mentioned nothing about it to us," he commented privately. "And we are so stubborn that had they mentioned it, we would not have dissolved it at all!" [8] The status of world Communism remained unchanged—a hint from the Kremlin was sufficient to discipline the most "independent" of the national parties—but the eclipse of a moribund bureaucracy that had long ceased to serve any revolutionary function could not have troubled Stalin, and it pleased public opinion in the Western democracies.

Russia's allies were heartened by the triumph at Stalingrad yet unable, except for the minor diversion in North Africa, to relieve the heavy burden on the Red Army. The long delayed second front on the Continent had been promised for 1943, but in June Roosevelt and Churchill decided that another postponement was necessary. Stalin's reproaches, though emphatic, became more dignified, probably because he realized that Russia could win the war without a major offensive by the West. His government, he wrote Churchill, "cannot become reconciled to this disregard of vital Soviet interests in the war against the common enemy. . . . [It] is not just the disappointment of the Soviet Government, but the preservation of its confidence in its Allies, a confidence which is being subjected to severe stress." [9]

For the balance of the summer relations were so strained that Washington and London feared a new Nazi-Soviet Pact might be in the making. A proposed Stalin-Roosevelt meeting was called off, the Soviet ambassador to London was recalled for "consultation," and Litvinov, appointed ambassador to Washington in 1942 as a symbol of Allied solidarity, was replaced by the embassy counselor. Further Russian victories and a successful Anglo-American campaign in Sicily helped to ease the tension. Stalin accepted the idea of a "Big Three" meeting, and in October a preliminary conference of foreign ministers convened in Moscow. Nothing of importance was accomplished, although Molotov spoke as if it were understood that Soviet interests would be paramount in eastern Europe after the war.

Late in November of 1943 Stalin, Roosevelt, and Churchill met for the first time in Teheran, the capital of Iran. Roosevelt, who stressed personal diplomacy, found Stalin "correct, stiff, solemn, not smiling"; there was "nothing human to get hold of." Seeking to penetrate the "icy surface," he teased Churchill unmercifully and succeeded in raising some hearty chuckles from Stalin. "Uncle Joe"—the affectionate diminutive for the Soviet ruler used within the Anglo-American entourage—had some flair for small talk and a surprising gift for repartee. When Churchill remarked, "I believe that God is on our side. At least I have done my best to make Him a faithful ally," Stalin grinned and added: "And the devil is on my side. Because, of course, everyone knows that the devil is a Communist and God, no doubt, is a good Conservative." [10]

The promise of a landing in France in 1944 was undoubtedly a more persuasive means of gaining Stalin's good will than any amount of friendly banter. He emphatically rejected Churchill's "soft underbelly" scheme—an attack on the Axis through the Mediterranean and the Balkans. It represented not only a dispersion of men and matériel from the major target but an unwarranted intrusion into southeastern Europe, an area that he had come to look upon as the Soviet Union's legitimate sphere of influence in the postwar world. The three leaders parted in a fraternal spirit on December 1.

Yet in spite of the surface camaraderie at Teheran there was no basis for a genuine understanding beyond the pressing requirements of a common war effort. As Stalin so succinctly put it, expressing the traditional view of beleaguered politicians: "In war I would deal with the devil and his grandmother." He continued to appraise his allies with cool cynicism. "Perhaps," he remarked to a Yugoslav Communist leader, "you think that just because we are the allies of the English that we have forgotten who they are and who Churchill is [Churchill had been the most prominent British advocate of intervention against Bolshevik Russia in 1919]. They find nothing sweeter than to trick their allies. During the First World War they constantly tricked the Russians and the French. And Churchill? Churchill is the kind who, if you don't watch him, will slip a kopeck out of your pocket. Yes, a kopeck out of your pocket! By God, a kopeck out of your pocket! And Roosevelt? Roosevelt is not like that. He dips in his hand only for bigger coins. But Churchill? Churchill—even for a kopeck." [11]

The Teheran Conference marked the high tide of Allied cooperation, for the complex political problems of the future were scarcely touched on. The most nagging of these issues was the Polish question. Soviet troops crossed Poland's pre-war frontier in January 1944, and the government-in-exile located in London promptly claimed the right to administer the liberated territory. Past relations between Moscow and the London Poles had been generally unpleasant despite mediation attempts by the British government, faced with the awkward dilemma of playing host to the dispossessed Poles and proving its fidelity to the Anglo-Soviet alliance. After the Katyn Forest incident of April 1943, in which the Poles lent credence to German charges that the Russians had massacred some 10,000 Polish officers near Smolensk in the spring of 1940, Moscow broke off diplomatic relations. Evidence available after the war upheld the Polish position—whether through error or deliberate policy the officers had indeed been killed while in Soviet custody—but the rupture was never healed.

Roosevelt and Churchill induced Stalin to see the Polish premier, Stanislaw Mikolajczyk, in August 1944, just as Polish underground troops—the so-called Home Army—rose in Warsaw against the Germans. The leaders hoped to liberate the city before the arrival of Soviet troops, then poised on the outskirts. The Russian offensive failed to materialize, however, and the Polish insurgents were compelled to appeal for outside aid. The Kremlin was backing its own Poles—the pro-Soviet Committee of National Liberation based in Lublin—and was loath to rescue a rival group. Stalin considered the "Warsaw adventure" a "reckless and fearful gamble" launched by a "handful of power-seeking criminals." But at length he yielded to insistent requests from his allies by allowing Soviet planes to drop supplies and by permitting a limited offensive. The remnants of the Home Army were nevertheless forced to surrender on October 2 after sixty-three days of the heroic but unequal struggle.

The disaster of the Warsaw uprising was a cruel blow to the Polish government-in-exile—the tragic climax to a losing fight with Russian power. Stalin had told Mikolajczyk that the London Poles would have to come to an agreement with the Lublin committee if they wanted representation in the new Poland. The premier was reluctant to do so and clung vainly to the hope that the Atlantic democracies would extract major concessions from the Kremlin. Stalin's callous indifference to the fate of the Home Army offered little reassurance that moral sentiment would carry any weight; and as the Red Army belatedly took Warsaw in January 1945, the available political leverage rapidly diminished.

One minor decision made at Teheran was to have unforeseen ramifications: the allies agreed to aid the Communist-led Partisans of Josip Broz—better known as Tito—rather than the Chetnik army of Drazha Mihailovich, a Serbian patriot backed by the Yugoslav government-in-exile. The Chetniks had adopted a passive attitude toward the occupation forces and sometimes collaborated to help stamp out Tito's Partisans. Insisting on a broad united front against the Axis, Stalin punctiliously abstained from supporting Communist guerrilla movements by word or deed. The Teheran decision made Tito respectable, and Soviet planes began dropping supplies in the spring of 1944. In September, as Soviet troops approached the Yugoslav border, Tito flew secretly to Moscow. There he met Stalin for the first time, and his independent attitude toward "the Boss" left the Soviet dictator's lieutenants aghast. Tito recalled that their initial conversation was "very cool," probably, he surmised, because of his censorious telegrams to Moscow earlier in the war, one of which had read: "If you cannot send us assistance, then at least do not hamper us." He was shocked and offended when Stalin spoke of the need to reinstate King Peter, then in exile. "You need not restore him forever," Stalin went on. "Take him back temporarily, and then you can slip a knife into his back at a suitable moment." [12] While their meetings were not an unqualified success, Stalin cooperated by sending Red Army units to help liberate Belgrade a few weeks later. The Soviet forces then withdrew for the invasion of Hungary, leaving Tito's new government in control of the country.

Stalin's willingness to reinstate the monarchy in Yugoslavia—a policy that bewildered Tito—was based on a tentative Anglo Soviet agreement on the Balkans arranged earlier in the summer. At opposite extremes in background and ideology, Stalin and Churchill found common ground in their political realism. The Nazi satellite empire was rapidly disintegrating, and Churchill did not propose to turn eastern Europe over to the Russians by default. Only two weeks after Tito's departure he arrived in Moscow for a conference with Stalin. At their first meeting the two leaders quickly agreed on a "percentage plan" to partition the Balkans between them: the Soviet Union to receive ninety per cent predominance in Romania and seventy-five per cent in Bulgaria; Britain to receive ninety per cent predominance in Greece; and the two countries to share equally in Yugoslavia and Hungary. The arrangement was rather pedantic in its arithmetical exactitude and lacked the permanence of a formal treaty, but the political implications were clear enough. Neither participant cared to probe too deeply into the other's interpretation of the agreement—"to let well alone," as Churchill put it.

Churchill left Moscow on October 19 with the feeling that his relations with Stalin had reached a new peak of amity. No unpleasantries marred the discussions as they ranged over a variety of topics, although the major achievement—the understanding on the Balkans—diminished in importance as the scope of American objections became clear. Meanwhile this Balkan entente paid a generous dividend to the West: Greece was firmly established as a British preserve.

As in Yugoslavia, a Communist-led Greek resistance movement —the E.A.M. or National Liberation Front—fought the Nazi authorities and won great popular support. With the Germans in full retreat in the fall of 1944, British troops landed with the exiled government of King George II in their wake. The "liberation" was obviously for political rather than military reasons. The E.A.M., allotted six cabinet posts in the new government, rejected as unfair the conditions under which its resistance forces were to disband. The Communist ministers resigned on December 1, and civil war soon broke out in Athens after the police fired on an unarmed group of E.A.M. demonstrators. A temporary truce was arranged in January 1945 when heavy British reinforcements bolstered the government's authority. Western liberals harshly attacked Churchill's strong-arm policy, but Stalin behaved with such impeccable restraint that Churchill paid him a grateful tribute: "Stalin . . . adhered strictly and faithfully to our agreement of October, and during all the long weeks of fighting the Communists in the streets of Athens not one word of reproach came from *Pravda* or *Isvestia*." [13]

Stalin was in no mood for revolutionary adventurism. Postwar security was his watchword. The Red Army crossed the pre-war frontiers of the Soviet Union not as zealots propagating the Communist gospel but as Tsarist troops had once marched into Napoleonic Europe. The only eager Communist missionaries were beyond Soviet jurisdiction: Mao Tse-tung, Tito, and the anonymous guerrillas of the French, Italian, and Greek resistance. Stalin either underestimated Communist opportunities—as in China—or sought to direct them into safe channels—as in Yugoslavia. A Russian nationalist in Marxist guise, he never quite understood that to the capitalist West Soviet power and Communism were identical. He had no such view himself. It was not the political dissembler speaking when he assured Mikolajczyk that Poland would remain a capitalist state because "Communism does not fit the Poles" and that "Communism on a German is like a saddle on a cow." [14] In the aftermath of the cold war his profoundly conservative role between 1944 and 1946 was blurred and forgotten in the West—if indeed it was ever really known.

The second Big Three conference took place in February 1945 at Yalta on the Crimean coast, once a vacation resort for Russian royalty. Germany's defeat, while not imminent, seemed inevitable enough to warrant an agenda largely composed of political items. The discussions were vigorous and only occasionally acrimonious. Stalin bargained stubbornly on issues that he deemed vital (e.g., Poland) but readily compromised on peripheral matters (e.g., the United Nations). As a weak substitute for realistic negotiations on eastern Europe, the United States produced a collection of hollow platitudes designed to encourage "democratic elements." Although neither Stalin nor Churchill could have taken the document seriously, this "Declaration on Liberated Europe" was duly signed.

The most significant agreement at Yalta was a secret pact insuring Soviet entry into the war against Japan. Roosevelt's military advisers predicted a million American casualties without Russian participation, and the price seemed cheap enough at the time: the restoration, in substance, of Russia's position in East Asia prior to the war with Japan in 1904–1905. Since Moscow was to regain its sphere of influence in Manchuria, Sino-Soviet negotiations took place during the summer. Stalin regarded Chiang as China's legitimate ruler; always skeptical of the Chinese Communists, he consistently discouraged Mao and his followers from pursuing their revolutionary aspirations.

Postwar disillusionment with Soviet policy, especially in the United States, focused popular attention on the Yalta Conference as a prime example of a "sellout" to Communist imperialism. But the legend bore no relation to reality. Stalin, too, made concessions and displayed a flexibility that was seldom duplicated in his remaining years. However painstakingly the Yalta record is scrutinized for clues to the future discord of the great powers, the conclusion is inescapable that the roots of Allied disunity lay elsewhere: the erosion of military necessity—always the best guarantor of unstable alliances—as victory approached in Europe; the hidden rivalry to fill the political vacuum left by a collapsing Germany; and the "normal" resurgence of ideological hostility between two disparate systems.

Within two weeks of the Yalta decisions Stalin dispatched Vyshinsky to Bucharest to bring Romania more securely into the Soviet fold. A pro-Communist coalition government was established under King Michael in response to Soviet pressure, and the United States lodged ineffective protests in Moscow. Churchill hung back, conscious of Stalin's circumspect attitude toward Greece and hopeful of a Polish settlement. The Yalta conferees had arranged an ethnically justifiable eastern frontier for Poland —the so-called Curzon line first proposed by the British in 1920. The more important question—who would rule Poland?—was concealed by an equivocal formula calling for a provisional government drawn from the Polish exiles and other non-Communist Poles and from Moscow's Lublin committee (already in effective control). A promise of Western-style elections was to legitimize the operation. To Churchill's complaint of a "veil of secrecy" being drawn over the Polish scene and to Roosevelt's challenge that "a thinly disguised continuance of the present Warsaw regime would be unacceptable," Stalin offered little more than a *fait accompli*. He would accept only "friendly" Poles who acknowledged the Curzon line and his interpretation of the Yalta accord.

Stalin also had a major grievance. When these polite recriminations were exchanged in April 1945 the war in Europe had yet to be won. The Red Army was encountering furious resistance in contrast to the token opposition offered the Anglo-American forces. Stalin regarded this behavior as "more than strange and unaccountable" in a message to Roosevelt and Churchill. The Germans "are fighting desperately . . . for Zemlenice, an obscure station in Czechoslovakia, which they need just as much as a dead man needs a poultice, but they surrender without any resistance such important towns in the heart of Germany as Osnabrück, Mannheim and Kassel." [15] He suspected his allies of arranging a secret understanding with Germany, and the exclusion of Soviet representatives from the projected surrender negotiations with the German command in Italy deepened his apprehension. Hitler still hoped to split the Allies by easing resistance on the western front, but the German fear of Communism, of Slavic "barbarism," and of the vengeful mood of the Russians were equally powerful motivations.

Stalin's distrust of his partners had been allayed somewhat—he "never doubted" their "integrity or trustworthiness"—when Roosevelt was fatally stricken on April 12. The emotional impact of the President's death briefly smoothed over the rift in Allied relations, and as a gesture of cooperation Stalin consented to send Molotov to the forthcoming organizational meeting of the United Nations in San Francisco. The new president, Harry S Truman, was more skeptical of Soviet intentions and lacked those genial personality traits that had helped his predecessor weld the coalition into an effective alliance.

Germany surrendered less than a month after Roosevelt's death. Japan's continued belligerence sustained but did not entirely preserve the façade of unity and good will among the victorious powers. Stalin had promised that the Soviet Union would attack Japan two or three months after Germany's capitulation. Despite Moscow's denunciation of its neutrality pact in April, Tokyo sought Russian mediation and offered a non-aggression pact in return for the evacuation and neutralization of Manchuria. By early summer Japan was too weak to bargain effectively— "angling in waters where no fish lived," as a Japanese diplomat wryly admitted. The United States, having developed an atomic bomb—not yet tested—grew more dubious about the necessity of Soviet assistance but stood by the Yalta agreement.

Various European problems, notably the perennial Polish question, had yielded grudgingly to the diplomatic finesse of Harry L. Hopkins, Truman's emissary, who conferred with Stalin in the Kremlin late in the spring. These preliminary negotiations thus secured a satisfactory climate for the last of the major wartime conferences. In July 1945 the Big Three met at Potsdam, the former residence of the Prussian kings near Berlin. Truman was determined to take a firm but reasonable stance, while Churchill, gloomily contemplating the expansion of Soviet power in Europe, espoused a tougher policy.

Stalin's aspirations may be plausibly surmised. That they then included a bloc of Communist states in eastern Europe is doubtful—not because his protestations to the contrary should be taken at face value but because of his actions. His insistence that the "Polish goose"—Churchill's phrase—be stuffed with German territory and that the Curzon line become Poland's eastern frontier; his demand for heavy reparations from Germany and her former tributary states; and his willingness to partition the Balkans all bespoke the language of nationalism, not of revolution. The hobbling of capitalist Germany to insure against future aggression was the key to his strategy in Europe, a far cry from Lenin's day when Germany had seemed the lodestar of world Communism. The Communist parties of the West were so lacking in revolutionary spirit that they verged on bourgeois respectability: in France, Italy, and Belgium they loyally participated in the postwar coalition governments. Stalin continued to expect Anglo-American recognition of Soviet influence in the East and to be deeply chagrined by the refusal of his allies to accept what he considered just recompense for the unparalleled sacrifices that the Russian people had made.

The major decisions at Potsdam involved Germany. The occupation zones had been previously arranged, and there was unanimous agreement on such matters as disarmament and de-Nazification. The Russians, already shipping industrial equipment to the Soviet Union as "war booty," were denied the $20,000,000,000 in reparations that Roosevelt had accepted at Yalta as a basis for discussion. They were to make good their claims in the Soviet occupation zone and to find additional compensation in the Western zones in exchange for raw materials. Thwarted on reparations, Stalin's position that the Polish-German frontier should be shifted westward to the Oder and Western Neisse rivers was accepted. Some nine million Germans had inhabited the area before the war, and the two million who had not already fled were evacuated. Since Poland already administered the territory, the pretense that a final disposition would be made at a formal peace conference hardly disguised the true nature of the transaction. Whatever the political complexion of the new Poland, its expansion at Germany's expense insured a common front with the Soviet Union on the boundary question.

Little else was accomplished at Potsdam beyond a spirited exchange of views on a larger variety of topics than the agenda had permitted at Yalta. Most of Stalin's proposals and complaints were tabled or referred to the Council of Foreign Ministers, an organization established at Potsdam to draft the peace treaties. Only a few, such as his request for a revision of the Straits convention, achieved a niche in the final protocol. The Western powers again registered strenuous objections to Soviet conduct in eastern Europe. Churchill protested to Stalin that their arrangement on Yugoslavia was not being kept, to which the latter replied that the Soviet government often did not know what Tito was up to. He added that "he had been hurt by the American demand for a change of Government in Rumania and Bulgaria" and regarded it as "unjust" because "he was not meddling in Greek affairs." [16]

Nothing was done at Potsdam to alter the political complexion of the developing Russian satellite empire. Indeed, nothing—or at least very little—could have been done, for moral suasion was useless and a show of force neither politically nor militarily feasible. The only practical alternative lay in exploring the possibilities presented by the Stalin-Churchill pact on the Balkans. Precisely the opposite course was pursued. Potsdam made it clear, if it had not been before, that the United States would never countenance spheres of influence in Europe. It seemed to Stalin that Britain was drawing closer to the American position. Certainly Churchill was beginning to have doubts about the scheme: he took as a sign of bad faith Stalin's inability to discipline Tito. Because the agreement had been personal and informal, Churchill's defeat at the polls during the conference aroused Soviet misgivings about the continuity of British policy. While neither country specifically disavowed the sphere arrangement, Potsdam marked an important way station in a general retreat from the supposed evils of power politics and secret diplomacy to a "democratic" concern for moral rectitude and hollow propaganda triumphs.

Japan's capitulation so soon after the Potsdam meeting would have seemed incredible a few weeks before. On July 16 Truman received word of the successful atomic bomb test in the New Mexico desert. Stalin was told of the new weapon after a week's delay but in such a cryptic manner that he apparently failed to grasp its full significance. Washington now regarded Soviet intervention as not only unnecessary but detrimental to American interests in the Far East. Determined to claim his rightful share of the spoils of victory, Stalin rushed preparations for a strike at Japan's dwindling power in Manchuria. On August 8, two days after Hiroshima had been obliterated by an atom bomb, the Red Army began a lightning campaign that pulverized the once formidable Kwantung Army within three weeks. The Russian defeat of 1904-

1905 had been revenged, a humiliation that according to Stalin "left bitter memories upon the people's conscience." His proclamation ignored the obvious: the bitterness had been directed against the Tsarist regime and not against Japan.

Stalin thus added the Far Eastern patrimony of Imperial Russia to his political and territorial gains in Europe. A national Communist estranged from his revolutionary origins, he never suspected that the status quo in Asia would be upset by his nominal disciples—the Chinese Communists. As in Europe, he was concerned with the traditional by-play of diplomacy and *Realpolitik,* too much the cynical realist to perceive the revolutionary currents which more than two decades of disappointment had taught him were mere figments of overwrought Marxist imaginations. It was left to Western commentators to enshrine the undeserving Stalin as a super-Machiavelli who could simultaneously aggrandize the Soviet state and nurture a revolution on the dimensions of the Chinese upheaval.

CHAPTER IX

The Return to Orthodoxy

THE WAR HAD AGED STALIN. RETOUCHED PHOTOGRAPHS RELEASED to the press gave an impression of mature vigor. But his neat and apparently bushy mustache had become scraggly and grey; his once firm torso had acquired an ungainly paunch; his hair was sparse, and his pasty complexion revealed long hours of sedentary labor in his Kremlin offices. Nor was his health good. He is said to have been stricken with a severe heart attack, probably in the fall of 1945, and allegedly suffered from several minor complaints.

Stalin's personal life continued to be shrouded in secrecy. Rosa Kaganovich, the handsome sister of his Politburo colleague Lazar Kaganovich and a physician by profession, was rumored to have become his third wife. But where and when the marriage ceremony took place—if indeed there were any formalities—is unknown. Vasily and Svetlana, the two children by his second wife, were now grown and married. His attitude toward them had alternated between tender solicitude and brusque severity, and on the rare occasions when they met family ties seemed unable to repair the estrangement of age and temperament. Vasily had become a lieutenant general in the air force during the war, largely on the strength of his name, and steadily degenerated into dipsomania and petty intrigue during the postwar years. He died at forty-one in 1962 after a strenuous drinking bout. Svetlana displayed greater emotional maturity than her brother despite two broken marriages. A fringe member of Moscow's literary intelligentsia, she was to become an international celebrity by defecting from the Soviet Union to the United States in 1967.

As an individual, Stalin was a remote paterfamilias to most Russians. Unlike Churchill, he seldom if ever toured the front or mingled with civilians to raise popular morale. He left the Kremlin infrequently during the early years of the war, and then usually on state business—the Teheran Conference or ceremonial appearances in Red Square. Occasionally he managed a brief respite at his dacha near Moscow, traveling in a limousine with elaborate security precautions. Yet despite his inaccessibility and deliberate aloofness, no Russian could be unaware of his symbolic presence. Slogans and portraits, busts and statues, press and radio had for years conveyed the message that every citizen knew by rote: the greatness, the wisdom, the magnanimity of Stalin. Although hundreds of thousands if not millions had personal reasons for despising him, the folk tradition of the good ruler surrounded by evil advisers persisted; nor did the overwhelming majority need reminding by the usual methods that he had led them to victory over the fascist invader. Never before or after was his prestige so great or his public esteem so high as on June 24, 1945, when he reviewed the conquering heroes of the Red Army from atop the Lenin mausoleum in Red Square.

If the emotions of an exhausted people gave undue and possibly undeserved credit to their leader, popular expectations had also been aroused to an exaggerated degree. Profound war weariness and unparalleled sacrifices of human and material resources led naturally to the assumption that such bloodshed and suffering could not have been in vain. Public opinion, insofar as it can be gauged, longed for a relaxation of the economic and political austerity of Stalinism. No one expected instant prosperity or a sudden eclipse of party controls, but it was not a mood that would have encouraged the leadership of a democratic country to demand more belt tightening and renewed vigilance against internal and external enemies of the state. This was essentially what Stalin did demand, though the restoration of Marxist orthodoxy from its wartime lapse was a gradual and relatively moderate process until the onset of the cold war.

Russia's losses in human lives—not counting the permanently maimed—may have exceeded the combined total of all the other combatants, including the victims of Nazi genocide policy. In 1946 Stalin gave a figure of seven million dead, a deliberate understatement to conceal the nation's manpower deficiency. More accurate estimates place the toll at close to twenty million, about three-fifths of which were civilian fatalities caused by enemy action, hunger, privation, and disease. The immediate problem was one of providing basic necessities, especially food and housing. Approximately a quarter of all Soviet property had been destroyed, and with the return of hordes of refugees and demobilized soldiers some twenty-five million persons were homeless. Caves, dugouts, and improvised shanties served as temporary shelters. The housing shortage, scandalous even before the war, was to plague the regime well beyond the Stalin era, but a building program, while entirely inadequate, alleviated the worst of the emergency by 1948.

The food shortage was somewhat less acute. Widespread famine was averted except for a severe drought in 1946 that caused starvation in parts of the Ukraine. But for the urban poor rationing restrictions and low agricultural productivity offered a monotonous diet at little better than a subsistence level. The encroachment of private garden plots on collective farm property and other illegal activities had been virtually ignored during the war. These abuses were curbed, and a more stringent policy toward the peasant, modified by appropriate incentives, failed to achieve production increases comparable to those of heavy industry. Agriculture continued to be the chronic invalid of the Soviet economy. But Stalin remained oblivious to the agrarian problem. "He knew the country and agriculture only from films," Khrushchev informs us. "And these films had dressed up and beautified the existing situation in agriculture. Many films so pictured *kolkhoz* [collective farm] life that the tables were bending from the weight of turkeys and geese. Evidently, Stalin thought that it was actually so."

The government launched a fourth Five Year Plan in March 1946. Stalin paid lip service to consumer needs, probably as a sop to public opinion, while assigning top priority to capital goods. He resented the "unfortunate and even brutal" manner in which Lend-Lease assistance had been terminated at the close of the European war; and Washington's disinterest in long term reconstruction credits confirmed his belief that the capitalist order was inherently hostile to Soviet socialism. On February 9, 1946, he signaled the return to Marxist fundamentals by proclaiming that the "capitalist system of world economy" concealed within itself the "elements of general crisis and military clashes." He called for a gigantic increase in steel, coal, and oil production to safeguard the country against "any accidents." [1] The stripping of East Germany and Manchuria of their industrial assets, a policy regarded in the West as ruthless looting, revealed the serious if not desperate straits of the economy. The party also maintained strict wartime labor discipline, and the forty-eight hour week, introduced in 1940, remained in effect.

The war had altered neither the political supremacy of the Communist party nor Stalin's control of the party machinery. Potential rivals—or at least alternative power structures—had nonetheless appeared because of the changing needs and functions of Soviet society: the government bureaucracy, whose duties and personnel had vastly expanded under Stalin, and the Red Army, whose generals were basically loyal to the regime but whose political outlook did not always coincide with that of the party. Since an interlocking directorate prevailed in the upper reaches of government and party—and both organs were subordinate to Stalin—a conflict of interest was not of grave concern. But Stalin never took chances. He was always alert to Bonapartist tendencies and ideological impurities. War prisoners and combat officers who had presumably been contaminated by Western attitudes while outside Soviet jurisdiction were subjected to political indoctrination. More serious cases of disaffection or suspected disloyalty were dealt with summarily: imprisonment or in some instances execution. This "purge of the heroes" was carried out secretly, and the number of middle echelon victims was perhaps greater than the more spectacular military purge of the 1930's. The famous commanders whose deeds had been celebrated—and sometimes exaggerated—for the sake of the war effort returned to the anonymity of routine service. Zhukov, the most illustrious of Stalin's marshals, was quietly relegated to an obscure post in Odessa.

The party had been enlarged by nearly two million members during the war. Admission standards were lowered in an attempt to broaden its base, and by 1945 the membership approached six million. Of those who survived the rigors of the war—and the casualty rate was particularly high among Communists—many of these new recruits were dropped for various deficiencies. Candidates were screened more carefully, and the party expanded at a less rapid pace, reaching almost seven million members in 1953 at the time of Stalin's death. The social composition of the party also changed. Theoretically an organization of the proletariat, it inevitably acquired an elitist character because of educational and other requirements. In the 1930's technical and administrative personnel had been enlisted in larger numbers, and this trend resumed in the postwar years even though "workers"— loosely defined—continued to predominate. But ordinary factory workers, as distinct from those with supervisory functions or special skills, became a decreasing minority. This partiality toward the new technical intelligentsia did not involve an increase in political sophistication. Aside from a superficial indoctrination in Marxist ideology, interpreted of course through the prism of Stalinist doctrine, the younger members lacked the revolutionary élan and the broader cultural background of the older generation. They did, however, acquire a taste for privilege, status, and "bourgeois" comforts as the standard of living improved. In time the social and psychological inroads of material affluence would erode the underpinnings of Stalin's totalitarian edifice, awaiting only the dictator's death for the seams and cracks to become visible.

Having cowed the party and reduced the Politburo and Central Committee to servile obedience during the Great Purge, Stalin took care that his lieutenants would not combine against him. By following the classic formula of divide and rule he succeeded in delegating authority without endangering his position; and the Politburo enjoyed greater stability during the last twenty years of his dictatorship than at any time before or after. The "old guard," whose elevation to the party's inner sanctum dated from at least 1930, comprised Kalinin (who died in 1946), Voroshilov, Molotov, and Kaganovich. Andrei Andreyev had been chosen in 1934, Anastas Mikoyan in 1935, Khrushchev in 1938, and Zhdanov in 1939. The newcomers were Beria and Malenkov (1946), Nikolai Voznesensky (1947), and Nikolai Bulganin and Alexei Kosygin (1948).

Zhdanov and Malenkov emerged after the war as Stalin's two most powerful subordinates. The latter's meteoric rise had somewhat overshadowed his senior colleague, and personal jealousy may have contributed to the political rivalry that sprang up between the two. Malenkov emerged the victor by default: Zhdanov died in 1948, apparently of a heart attack. Because a drastic purge followed in the Leningrad party organization—Zhdanov's fiefdom since the assassination of Kirov—unconfirmed rumors of foul play arose. Malenkov seems to have taken the initiative in this mystifying "Leningrad Affair," though whether he acted at Stalin's prompting or simply with his consent is unclear. Zhdanov's protégé, Voznesensky, disappeared in 1949, and a similar fate befell hundreds of highly placed party officials in the Leningrad area. Many, including Voznesensky, were executed while in custody and others dispatched to labor camps. No public charges were leveled against these supposed Zhdanovites, and Zhdanov's memory remained unsullied by posthumous recriminations. In many respects the Leningrad Affair bore a curious resemblance to the Kirov assassination and the prelude to the Great Purge. Perhaps Stalin nourished a permanent grudge against Russia's most cosmopolitan city as a cesspool of subversion and nonconformity.

By late 1948 Malenkov had secured a dominant position in the party Secretariat and was without a serious competitor as heir apparent to the aging Stalin. But a year later Khrushchev, who had made his reputation as the party boss of the Ukraine, was appointed first secretary of the Moscow organization and assigned to the Secretariat of the Central Committee. While not immediately as formidable an opponent as Zhdanov, he superseded Andreyev as the Politburo's agricultural specialist and clearly ranked just below Malenkov in the party hierarchy. His plan to reduce the number of collective farms in order to raise their efficiency and simplify the problem of political control was carried out in Stalin's last years. By 1953 the number of collectives had been reduced from approximately 250,000 to 94,000. His ambitious scheme to build "agro-towns" for the peasantry ran into opposition from Malenkov and Beria—among others—and Stalin ended the dispute by siding with them.

Of those Politburo members whose principal duties lay outside the party apparatus, the most influential were probably Molotov, Beria, and Bulganin. The dour and colorless Molotov continued to enjoy Stalin's confidence after the war and was as close to intimacy with the *Vozhd* as anyone from his political entourage ever became. Until 1949, when he was replaced as foreign minister, his sphere of activity necessarily kept him on the periphery of major domestic issues. The loss of his cabinet post was not formally intended as a demotion—Politburo members were divested of ministerial responsibility to allow more time for general policy decisions. Yet Molotov seems to have been downgraded thereafter; certainly his relationship with Stalin deteriorated, and his wife, Plina Zhemchuzhina, served a term in prison.

Beria controlled, at least nominally, not only the vast empire of the secret police but important segments of the economy, notably the development of atomic energy. That he too had fallen out of favor by 1951 is suggested by the arrest of various Georgian officials with whom he was politically linked. Bulganin, originally a disciple of Kaganovich, acted as Stalin's trouble-shooter during the war and replaced Voroshilov on the State Committee for Defense in 1944. An experienced "political general," he became minister of the armed forces and marshal of the Soviet Union after the war. By 1950, if not earlier, he had supplanted Voroshilov as the chief liaison between the Politburo and the military establishment. Stalin, Khrushchev informs us, "toyed . . . with the absurd and ridiculous suspicion that Voroshilov was an English agent," and for "several years he was actually deprived of the right of participation in Political Bureau sessions." [2]

Voroshilov was spared the fate of Voznesensky, nor did he share the public humiliation of Andreyev, who was denounced in a *Pravda* article in 1950 for his views on collective farm management and likewise prevented from attending Politburo meetings. Stalin's capriciousness increased as he grew older, and given more time he would have made a clean sweep of his associates, assuredly those of the older generation. All of them, Khrushchev suggests, were in danger of "future annihilation." In these last years no plenary sessions of the Central Committee were held, and the Politburo, which met infrequently at irregular intervals, had already been crippled as a collective party organ by Stalin's haphazard practice of creating committees among its members to deal with separate problems.

"The cult of the individual," according to Khrushchev, "acquired such monstrous size chiefly because Stalin himself, using all conceivable methods, supported the glorification of his own person." The official "short biography" appearing in 1948 reached a new peak of "loathsome adulation," in part because Stalin was not wholly satisfied with his sycophants and appended to the manuscript several repellent examples of self-congratulation. Stalin wrote about himself: "Although he performed his task of leader of the party and the people with consummate skill and enjoyed the unreserved support of the entire Soviet people, Stalin never allowed his work to be marred by the slightest hint of vanity, conceit, or self-adulation." He considered another passage, "Stalin is the Lenin of today," too weak and changed it to read: "Stalin is the worthy continuer of Lenin's work, or, as it is said in our party, Stalin is the Lenin of today." [3] It was once maintained by the dictator's apologists abroad that he never really enjoyed the sickening flattery that was showered upon him but that he endured it as a politic means of gaining mass support for his program. A more likely explanation is that he had—or acquired—an insatiable craving for the most blatant forms of personal tribute. His self-esteem required constant approbation as an alcoholic demands liquid stimulation.

The inflexibility of Stalin's political regimen was matched by a stifling cultural orthodoxy that surpassed the obscurantist legacy of the 1930's. To the old blend of Marxist ideology and Stalinist dogma a new ingredient was added: Soviet-style xenophobia. The wartime amalgam of Soviet patriotism and Russian nationalism was not permitted to lapse. Stalin even flirted with Great Russian chauvinism, praising the Russian people as the "most outstanding nation of all the nations within the Soviet Union." He suspected with good reason that the national minorities were at best apathetic toward his regime. Some of the smaller nationalities—the Volga Germans, the Crimean Tartars, the Kalmyks, and several Caucasian peoples—were deported to Siberia and Central Asia during the war, unfairly accused of collective disloyalty. Had it been practicable the huge Ukrainian population of some forty million would also have been sent into internal exile.

In Lenin's time nationalism, except as an adjunct to the struggle for liberation against colonial rule, had been labeled a manifestation of bourgeois ideology. Stalin not only abandoned this seemingly immutable Marxist principle but enlisted the "new" Soviet nationalism for double duty—as a weapon against the Western bourgeoisie and as an instrument to rally the people to the Communist state. Capitalist civilization was not simply decadent, as the Kremlin's propagandists had long maintained, it was demonstrably inferior when compared to the Russian past and the Soviet present. In its extreme form the argument was patently ridiculous, and the attempt to establish Russian supremacy retroactively in almost every field from sport to the printing press further alienated Western opinion and mortified the more perceptive among Soviet intellectuals. Although Stalin never mastered popular psychology as he did the mechanics of political power, he managed, however crudely, to develop a sense of pride and accomplishment among a substantial portion of the people. But he failed to instill more than a superficial hostility toward the West, most likely because of the universal dread of a new war and a feeling that the Soviet Union was in no immediate danger of an attack.

To a great extent the renewed drive for intellectual conformity served as a barometer of the cold war. Its most intense phase, the so-called *Zhdanovshchina,* was associated with the pronouncements of Stalin's chief ideologue Andrei Zhdanov during the late forties when Soviet-Western relations reached a peak of tension. Zhdanov's premature death scarcely interrupted the party's cultural offensive, though the vigor of the assault was somewhat diffused. No significant relaxation was permitted until Stalin himself was safely in his grave.

A decree on literature issued by the Central Committee in August 1946 launched the party's campaign for ideological purity. Two literary journals published in Leningrad were denounced for their "art for art's sake" approach and their "servility to the contemporary bourgeois culture of the West." The satirist Mikhail Zoshchenko and the poet Anna Akhmatova were specifically reprimanded for their "empty, trivial works, without content and pervaded by a rotten lack of ideas and political indifference, calculated to disorganize our youth and poison its consciousness." [4] Another decree censured the dramatists for their failure to present the Soviet people in a more positive light and condemned the performance of "bourgeois" plays by Western dramatists. In September, Zhdanov clarified these general guidelines in lengthy speeches to the writers and party workers of Leningrad. Since the "imperialists" were mounting an ideological onslaught, he maintained, it was the duty of Soviet writers not only to answer these slanders but to attack bourgeois culture, already in "a state of disintegration and decay."

Stalin remained publicly aloof from the controversy while retaining his keen interest in all aspects of cultural "partyness" and exercising his customary supervision over the actions of his subordinates. He prided himself on his knowledge of Russian and Soviet literature, and one of his witticisms has been recorded about a book of love poems by Konstantin Simonov: "They should have published only two copies—one for her, and one for him!" He remained a friend of the literary classics, with the major exception of Fyodor Dostoyevsky. "A great writer," he admitted, "and a great reactionary. We are not publishing him because he is a bad influence on the youth. But, a great writer!" [5]

The party soon extended the struggle for Bolshevik orthodoxy to the creative arts and several fields of scholarship. The film industry came under fire for its negativism, and the internationally famous director Sergei Eisenstein was reproved for an insufficiently "progressive" view of Ivan the Terrible. The staging of a new opera by Vano Muradeli in February 1948 occasioned a Central Committee resolution attacking "formalism" in music and rebuking such outstanding composers as Dmitri Shostakovich and Sergei Prokofiev. They were ordered, in effect, to avoid the decadent influence of Western bourgeois music and to find their inspiration in folk melodies and the conventional themes bequeathed by the great classical composers.

History and the social sciences were already so thoroughly regimented that the party bloodhounds failed to turn up significant departures from accepted political norms. The one major exception, Eugene Varga's study of capitalism, contended that an economic crisis in the West could be postponed for at least a decade and that the contradictions inherent in the capitalist system would not inevitably lead to war. The thesis unwittingly countered Stalin's assumptions about the postwar world, and Voznesensky, himself a professional economist, was chosen to lead the chorus of abuse in the spring of 1947. Varga lost his most prestigious post but was not personally molested, nor was he obliged to undergo more than token "self-criticism." Obviously there was disagreement in the Politburo which Stalin did not choose to resolve by drastic action.

Georgi Aleksandrov's *History of Western European Philosophy* became a scapegoat in August 1947 for Zhdanov's further strictures on the state of Soviet ideology. Aleksandrov had supposedly slighted the history of Russian philosophy and set a poor example on the "philosophical front," where action was needed to counter the "pimps and depraved criminals" serving as philosophers in the United States and Britain. He was dismissed as deputy director of the Central Committee's *Agitprop* section but, like Varga, continued his career in a humbler capacity.

Science, except in the case of biology and physiology, had been all but immune from confrontation with the guardians of the party's intellectual salubrity. Its privileged position was weakened to some extent in 1949–1950 when the more zealous propagandists sought to link dialectical materialism with mathematics and the natural sciences and to demonstrate that Soviet science was somehow more "progressive" than that of the capitalist countries. Even astronomers were exhorted to fight against "bourgeois cosmology" as a manifestation of the "reactionary science" of the West. But this type of chauvinism had little practical impact on the scientists themselves, and in most fields basic research as well as its technological offspring proceeded unhindered. Albert Einstein's theory of relativity, out of favor for a time, again became respectable in 1951. Lysenko—the "Savonarola of Soviet science"—ruled more securely as the arbiter of Soviet biology after a notable debate in 1948 at the Academy of Agricultural Sciences. Twelve leading biologists were dismissed from their university and government positions for differing with the party mandate supporting Lysenko.

During the late forties the stock phrases of published invective —"rootless cosmopolitans" and "passportless tramps"—were applied to a disproportionate number of Jews, a covert expression of anti-Semitism partly traceable to Stalin's personal views. Attacks on "Zionism," seemingly a more respectable substitute for outright propaganda against Jews, pervaded the party press. "The entire older generation is contaminated with Zionism," Stalin complained to his daughter, "and now they're teaching the young people, too." [6] Jews had been prominent among the Old Bolsheviks, and in the highest reaches of the party only Kaganovich—certainly a very Russified Jew—had survived the Great Purge. Unofficial discrimination against Jews, especially in the party and some professions, developed after the war, possibly a partial response to popular anti-Semitism. In 1949 public manifestations of Yiddish culture—books, periodicals, and the theater—were suppressed, and scores of Jewish intellectuals were imprisoned or executed. The fate of some three million Soviet Jews seemed to be hanging in the balance during the last years of Stalin's rule.

The only instance in which Stalin openly intervened to settle an intellectual controversy involved the linguistics debate of 1950. The views of Nikolai Marr, a philologist who died in 1934, had hitherto prevailed as the orthodox Marxist interpretation of language development. He contended that language, like art, religion, politics, and law, was a by-product of economic forces and class relationships. A universal language would evolve once world Communism had been achieved. In choosing to refute Professor Marr, Stalin broke an extended silence which, apart from interviews, ceremonial remarks, and written answers to questions posed by foreign correspondents, had lasted well over four years. His ten thousand word essay entitled "Marxism and Problems of Linguistics" filled a good half of the June 20 issue of *Pravda,* and was supplemented by later pronouncements. Conceding his amateur standing as a philologist, he nevertheless demolished the "Marrists" to his own satisfaction. He associated them with vulgar Marxists—the "Troglodytes"—whose dogmatism and pedantry had nothing in common with true Marxism. On the one hand he seemed to be an apostle of liberalism, implying that the party's rigid control of the nation's intellectual life had gone too far; on the other, he spoke as an unreconstructed nationalist, hinting that the international language of the future would be Russian, not Marr's hypothetical "language of socialism."

This ambiguous and prolix excursion into linguistic theory baffled party spokesmen as well as foreign observers. Like the revelations of a modern Delphic oracle, Stalin had become too enigmatic for even the Stalinists to explicate the sacred text with confidence. If it was a signal for ideological moderation, it was muted and entirely too subtle for the party to act. The hounds of heresy were not called off, although Stalin was more concerned with political than doctrinal deviation during his final years.

CHAPTER X

The Cold War

MANY WESTERNERS—PERHAPS A MAJORITY OF AMERICANS—TOOK IT for granted that the cold war arose full blown from Stalin's malevolent brain. His contribution was substantial, of course, for without his malignant presence Soviet relations with the Atlantic democracies would scarcely have degenerated to the level that prevailed during his declining years.

The disintegration of the grand alliance and the onset of mutual hostility so soon after the Axis defeat could not be readily assimilated by public opinion. Alternative "conspiracy" theories arose to explain a complex process in one-dimensional terms. In the West the basic difficulty was ascribed to Communist aggression. The Soviet Union had embarked on a program of world conquest: eastern Europe was engulfed in the Red empire, and proxy armies—notably that of the Chinese Communists—were bent on a similar mission in East Asia. The Kremlin's political ambitions and doctrinal aims were consistently confused with military objectives. Misunderstanding the nature of the Soviet threat, the Western powers reacted with a collective will and purpose more appropriate to the 1930's. The lessons that history can teach were learned—too late and in the wrong context.

In the Soviet Union the roots of the growing antagonism were traced to capitalist imperialism. The insatiable drive for international markets, a surplus of investment capital accumulated by war profiteers, the threat of recurring economic crises bred by the inequities of capitalist society: these were the realities that masked hypocritical prating about "democracy" and "freedom" as the United States assumed the economic and political assets of the floundering British Empire and mounted an offensive against Soviet socialism. This was Stalin's style of primitive Marxism—grafted, unfortunately, to an increasingly xenophobic strain of Russian nationalism.

The arguments of the opposing sides were not without merit, although the propaganda content designed for popular consumption was obviously high. Soviet expansion did indeed imperil the traditional European balance of power; but the United States, in "containing" the danger, succumbed to the temptation of a moral crusade against Communism, leading inevitably to an open-ended global conflict that bore only a faint relationship to the original goal. As "superpowers" thrust into an unaccustomed role by the Axis collapse and the decay of Britain and France as great powers, they confronted each other as alien behemoths, each espousing contradictory ideologies, political systems, and national interests. In less dramatic form the cold war had been endemic if not continuous since November 1917, and the wartime coalition could be interpreted as a temporary suspension of a "normal" condition.

The seriousness of the East-West estrangement in the latter half of 1945 was concealed from the general public, partly by governmental secrecy and partly by popular good will that refused to accept former allies as potential menaces to postwar peace and stability. No diplomatic incidents had yet marred the outward serenity of international relations. But the divergence of Soviet and Western interests at Potsdam had been an ominous portent, and the failure of the Council of Foreign Ministers, meeting in London in the early fall of 1945, confirmed the growing dissension. The representatives could not even agree on a communiqué for the press.

The underlying issue remained the Western refusal to acknowledge Soviet preponderance in eastern Europe. The United States, with Britain's adherence, insisted on the letter of the Yalta declaration regarding the liberated territories and clung to the ritualistic formula of governments "both friendly to the Soviet Union and representative of all the democratic elements of the country." The statement was patently contradictory. A democratic government in the Western sense could hardly satisfy the Soviet or any reasonable definition of "friendly." (Finland was to become the exception that proved the rule.) Nor did the prospects for democracy in an economically backward area whose population had never known civil liberties, an effective parliament, or a fluid social order seem to trouble Washington and London. The Russians could not openly admit their unpopularity either as Communists or as imperialists despite Stalin's blunt statement at Potsdam that "a freely elected government in any of these countries would be anti-Soviet, and that we cannot allow." [1] But they suspected with good reason that it was not so much the state of democracy in eastern Europe that the West found objectionable as the expansion of Soviet power far beyond the geographical and political expectations of Tsarist Russia.

The collapse of the London conference of the foreign ministers induced both Moscow and Washington to make conciliatory gestures. The United States recognized the provisional governments of Austria and Hungary, and the Soviet Union reciprocated by allowing free elections in both countries. The returns revealed such unexpected Communist weakness—the party polled seventeen per cent of the vote in Hungary and only five per cent in Austria—that Stalin declined thereafter to permit the electorate a free choice within the Soviet sphere of influence. The Moscow meeting of the Council of Foreign Ministers (December 1945), by avoiding the difficult question of the European peace treaties and by compromising several minor problems, offered renewed hope that the estrangement between East and West was only temporary.

It was not in Europe but in the Middle East that the general public—at least in the West—first became aware of the nascent conflict. Allied troops, including those of the Red Army, still occupied Iran, and the Russians supported a separatist movement under the leadership of Iranian Communists. Stalin's tactics were unnecessarily clumsy: oil concessions, not territorial aggrandizement, was his goal. In January 1946 Iran appealed to the newly organized United Nations because of Soviet interference, and what should have been a relatively minor dispute was blown up into an international crisis. Stalin procrastinated about withdrawing his forces on schedule, inducing an Anglo-American protest; the Soviet representative walked out of a Security Council session in March, an irritating display of bad manners; and in the spring Moscow and Teheran reached an independent settlement, including an oil agreement. In the end, however, the Russians had nothing to show for their boorish conduct, for Iran's attitude stiffened with the evacuation of Soviet troops, and Washington jettisoned its lingering inhibitions about diplomatic and financial support to the embattled Iranians.

Winston Churchill's celebrated "Iron Curtain" speech in Fulton, Missouri, on March 5 overshadowed the Iranian controversy. As a "private citizen" he could articulate serious misgivings about Soviet policy that public officials fully shared on both sides of the Atlantic. The occasion marked the ideological beginning of the cold war, though in retrospect the speech would seem almost timid beside the frenzied recriminations that were to follow. The

Soviet press and its Communist auxiliaries elsewhere took up the challenge, and Stalin entered the lists with a vehement rebuke to his wartime colleague: Churchill and his associates "bear a striking resemblance to Hitler and his friends"; and if they should succeed in organizing a "new military expedition against eastern Europe," then "one can confidently say that they will be beaten, just as they were beaten twenty-six years ago." Stalin's resentment was also expressed to the new American ambassador, General Walter Bedell Smith, when he was received in the Kremlin for the first time. To Smith's query, "Is it possible that you really believe that the United States and Great Britain are united in an alliance to thwart Russia?" Stalin responded with a curt "Yes." [2]

What the Soviet dictator might permit himself in private could not be said in public. The propaganda media were still restrained in their comment on Western policy, an attitude reciprocated by the "Establishment" in Washington and London. For the balance of the year the two blocs kept up the pretense that while relations were troubled there were no immutable barriers to a permanent understanding.

The debating habits and diplomatic etiquette of the Soviet representatives had meanwhile grown steadily more discourteous. Nor did they have freedom of initiative. At the United Nations and its various bodies, at the Allied Control Council for Germany and its innumerable committees, and at the Council of Foreign Ministers their position, even on trivial matters, was usually inflexible because of rigid instructions from the Kremlin. Molotov, whose only effective superior was Stalin himself, set the pattern by his churlish behavior and peevish obstinacy. At the Paris meeting of the Council of Foreign Ministers in the spring of 1946 the United States proposed, and the other powers accepted, a change in the press rules to give full publicity to the proceedings. The Council rostrum was rapidly transformed into a propaganda medium: open quarrels, openly arrived at, henceforth became the fashion in great power negotiations as well as in the United Nations.

At the beginning of 1947 neither Russia nor the United States was willing to admit that their mounting antagonism had reached a point of no return. Peace treaties with the minor Axis nations finally had been hammered out, and there was cautious optimism that the more onerous task of drafting treaties with Germany and Austria might be completed during the course of the year. Stalin's German policy, aside from the immediate aim of securing reparations and the long range objective of rendering the late enemy incapable of future aggression, reflected his preference for economic reform by political fiat. Indifferent to the Western remedy for political ills—civil liberties and free elections —he introduced drastic changes in a social order that had remained almost intact since the Kaiser's day. Bank accounts were frozen, key industries nationalized, and land reform introduced. The forced dissolution of the great Junker estates strengthened the small farmers and provided a livelihood for German refugees expelled from eastern Europe. It was in no sense a Communist program. As a Red Army officer so forcefully put it: "Give Communism to such swine? . . . We certainly don't intend to bring a noble ideal like Communism to such a people." [3] The eradication of Nazism, pursued vigilantly throughout Germany, became a kind of political crusade in the Soviet zone without the judicial restraints found in the west. Yet the Russians did not hesitate to employ former Nazis if their knowledge or skills proved useful.

German Communism had been virtually exterminated during the Nazi era, and of those who escaped to Soviet exile many had perished in Stalin's purge of foreign Communists. One of the survivors, Wilhelm Pieck, was dispatched from Moscow to assume the party leadership in 1945. The Social Democrats merged with the Communists in April 1946, and by 1947 the hybrid Socialist Unity party became wholly subordinate to Moscow's will. What popular following the party acquired gradually fell away as its puppet status became clear and the repressive features of the East German regime intensified with the progress of the cold war.

The Truman Doctrine and the Marshall Plan, both promulgated by Washington in 1947, demolished the shaky pretense that the differences of the preceding two years had been a quirk of fate, a series of misunderstandings that patience and good will would rectify. They demonstrated to Stalin's satisfaction that the United States had become a serious competitor in Europe and the Middle East. President Truman's decision in March to assist Greece and Turkey—"to support free peoples . . . resisting attempted subjection by armed minorities or by outside pressure" —was prompted by Britain's inability to maintain her imperial interests in the eastern Mediterranean. In 1946 civil war had again broken out in Greece. The Balkan pact with Churchill had already lapsed by default, but Stalin displayed a curious indifference toward the Greek Communists, whose guerrilla forces were given sanctuary and supplies by Yugoslavia, Bulgaria, and Albania. Stalin distrusted Communists not under his supervision, and the Greek party had few if any direct ties with Moscow. "They have no prospect of success at all," he told a Yugoslav delegation in January 1948. "What do you think, that Great Britain and the United States—the United States, the most powerful state in the world—will permit you to break their lines of communication in the Mediterranean Sea! Nonsense. And we have no navy. The uprising in Greece must be stopped, and as quickly as possible." [4]

Soviet ambitions toward Turkey rested upon the historic tradition of Turkish debility and Russian aggrandizement. Stalin felt that the Straits convention of 1936 was no longer appropriate to his nation's new stature in international affairs, and he also claimed some Transcaucasian territory ceded to Turkey after World War I. Soviet propaganda attacks were augmented by troop movements, fleet maneuvers in the Black Sea, and border violations. The seriousness of Moscow's intentions may be doubted, for the Turkish Straits were no longer of vital strategic concern in an age of air power. As in Iran, Stalin sought unilateral negotiations without Western interference and probably would have settled for much less than his full demands. Again he overplayed his hand and curtailed his diplomatic gamesmanship when American assistance for the Turks materialized.

Stalin's initial response to the Marshall Plan was wary but almost friendly compared to his reception of the Truman Doctrine. Designed to alter the image of power politics and "blank check" anti-Communism implicit in Truman's policy, the Marshall Plan comprised a long range program of economic aid to help achieve European recovery. The Russians decided to explore the possibility of cooperation, and Molotov headed a large delegation for a preliminary meeting in Paris. Fearing American interference in East Europe, he spurned an itemized survey to determine Europe's economic needs and proposed that each country submit a "shopping list" to Washington. Before the Soviet attitude could be fully explored Stalin recalled the delegation to Moscow.

Soviet propaganda rode the theme of American economic imperialism, with a subsidiary refrain that the Marshall Plan was designed to avert a new depression in the United States. Poland, among Moscow's dependencies, was eager to share in Washington's largesse, and Czechoslovakia prepared to send representatives to a conference on July 12. Stalin confronted the Czech leaders in the Kremlin and told them the facts of political life. Jan Masaryk, returning to Prague, confided his bitterness to a friend: "I went to Moscow as the Foreign Minister of an independent sovereign state; I returned as a lackey of the Soviet Government." [5] Unable to provide a substitute for the Marshall Plan, the Soviet government improvised a series of trade pacts—dubbed the "Molotov Plan" in the West—that did little more than point toward economic self-sufficiency within the Soviet orbit.

Convinced of the hostile intent of the United States, Stalin rang down the Iron Curtain with a vengeance. Soviet domination of eastern Europe, concealed but effective, no longer sufficed. There were to be no weak links in the chains that bound the vassal states to the Communist fatherland. Political dissenters were purged and "Muscovites"—Moscow-trained Communists whose loyalty to Stalin was unquestioned—given preference over wartime resistance leaders. Not only was Western influence excluded; the prospect of "different roads to socialism" was extinguished. Fraud, coercion, and violence were the conventional weapons of political combat. For the great mass of passive citizens, who cherished no deep commitment to Western-style democracy, Communist leadership offered substantial rewards: social welfare services, land reform, educational opportunities, and full employment. And there was always the promise of a better life in the future. But the forces of nationalism were never expunged, and Stalin's tested methods—essentially the carrot and stick approach—failed to engender popular enthusiasm for the socialist millennium.

Poland's subordination was particularly galling to the Western powers because of the protracted struggle with Stalin to erect a genuine coalition government. By 1946 most anti-Communists had rallied to Mikolajczyk's Peasant party as the focus of the opposition. The parliamentary election in January 1947 was a travesty of the electoral process. The government's "Democratic bloc" claimed a sweeping victory, and Mikolajczyk fled the country nine months later to avoid arrest. The Peasant party, thoroughly "disciplined," joined the coalition. With the forced merger of the Social Democrats and Communists late in 1948 the last vestige of legal opposition was eradicated.

In Hungary the Smallholders party, after winning the free election held in November 1945, shared power with the Communists. Like the Polish Peasant party, the Smallholders were subjected to harassing tactics that culminated in the arrest of its leaders and the forced resignation of Premier Ferenc Nagy in May 1947. A new election, with various impediments to a free expression of opinion, returned a Communist plurality. In 1948 the opposition parties were eliminated in piecemeal fashion. The last important holdout, the Social Democrats, were absorbed by the Communists in June.

The pattern in neighboring Romania varied only sightly. Since Vyshinsky had done his work well in 1945, strong-arm methods were less blatant. A rigged election in November 1946 produced a huge majority for the pro-Communist government slate. In July 1947 the National Peasant party was banned after an alleged conspiracy against the state, and the Liberals were forced out of the cabinet in November. The monarchy, having become a useless anachronism, gave way to a republic as King Michael was forced to abdicate. A new election in March 1948 insured an overwhelming vote for the government candidates.

Bulgaria's traditional friendship with Russia eased the Communist road to total power. A suspect election in November 1945 had confirmed the authority of the Fatherland Front, originally an anti-Nazi underground organization. Communists held the key ministries and gradually extended their control. Georgi Dimitrov, who had spent many of his years of exile in Moscow, became premier in November 1946. The Agrarian party was dissolved in 1947 after the execution of its leader, Nikola Petkov, on flimsy charges of subversion. A year later the arrest and imprisonment of Kosta Lulchev and other prominent Socialists subdued the last competitor to Communist rule through the agency of the Fatherland Front.

Western opinion was aroused but not unduly alarmed by the Communist subjugation of eastern Europe. The process lacked the dramatic impact of a coup d'état or a popular revolution, and many had already conceded the area as a Soviet preserve. The fall of Czechoslovakia to Communism was an entirely different matter. The Czechs were proud of their unique status as a neutral bridge between the Communist East and the capitalist West, and the surprisingly large Communist vote in May 1946—thirty-eight per cent, a clear plurality—reflected the traumatic shock of the Munich betrayal and the Red Army's role in liberating the country from the Nazi yoke. The coalition government increased its Communist representation, and party chief Klement Gottwald became the new premier. Stalin seemed content with the status quo until the Marshall Plan incident. Thereafter the Communists prepared a "legal" seizure of power through their control of the Interior Ministry and its security forces. In February 1948 twelve non-Communists resigned from the cabinet in protest, an act of self-immolation since the government spurned the accepted rules of parliamentary procedure. Valerian Zorin, the Soviet deputy foreign minister, flew to Prague in the midst of the crisis. He told Masaryk that the Kremlin was gravely concerned by the rise of "reactionary" elements in Czechoslovakia and intimated that the Soviet government might find it necessary to intervene. "Loyal" police moved into the capital, armed workers under Communist leadership paraded through the streets, and "subversives" were rounded up. President Eduard Benes, as commander-in-chief, could have called on the army but preferred to avoid the risk of civil war. A new cabinet reorganization gave only token representation to the minor parties, though Masaryk and Benes temporarily retained their posts. The tragic death of Masaryk—a supposed suicide—symbolized for many Czechs the end of an era that had begun almost four decades before with his father, the great "president-liberator" Thomas G. Masaryk.

The destruction of Czech democracy came as a numbing shock to the Atlantic community. Although Stalin was now satisfied with his Berlin-Prague-Vienna picketline, Communist strength in France and Italy—not to mention its resurgence in Asia—brought renewed fears of Soviet sorties beyond the Iron Curtain. Stalin's strategy of concealed aggression was a triumph of political technique, but in flouting national tradition by importing an alien sytem Stalinism carried the seeds of its own destruction. If the old tyrant did not live to see its disintegration, he witnessed the first signs of rebellion, and for once he was unable to crush the heretics by excommunication or intimidation. These premature anti-Stalinists were the Yugoslav Communists. As unpunished and unrepentant schismatics they were a far greater threat to the mother church of Communism than if they had been capitalist infidels.

Before the rupture between Stalin and Tito, Yugoslavia had been accorded a place of honor in the Communist hierarchy second only to the Soviet Union. Stalin personally selected Belgrade as headquarters for the Communist Information Bureau (Cominform), an association of European Communist parties secretly organized in Poland in September 1947. Its avowed purpose was informational and propagandist; its actual function was to act as a transmission belt for Soviet directives, particularly to insure orthodoxy among the satellites and to prod the French and Italian Communists into militant action against Marshall Plan aid. Stalin devised the cumbrous title of the Cominform journal—*For a Lasting Peace, For a People's Democracy!*—on the theory that the Western press would have to repeat the slogan in quoting from it. But his ingenuity was circumvented: "the organ of the Cominform" became the standard nomenclature. He took an active interest in censoring and otherwise molding the journal's contents, leaving the managing editorship to Paul Yudin, one of his most servile "philosophers."

The roots of Tito's defection lay in the independent and indigenous development of Yugoslav Communism. The party leaders, while innocent of any conscious deviation from Communist purity, had not been handpicked by Stalin and had made their own revolution without significant help from the Red Army. Until 1948 there was little to distinguish the Yugoslav regime from its Balkan counterparts except that the pretense of coalition government was discarded before the end of 1945. Tito was a Communist dictator—but an uncommonly popular one compared to the Soviet puppets who ruled in Warsaw, Bucharest, Sofia, and Budapest. Even Stalin could not have attracted the enthusiastic crowds that greeted Tito on his state visits to the satellite capitals.

The petty irritations that aggravated Moscow's "fraternal" relationship with Belgrade could have been smoothed over with tactful diplomacy. But Stalin had grown so accustomed to unquestioned obedience from subordinates that the slightest opposition infuriated him. From his point of view he treated the Yugoslavs with unusual deference. He urged them, for example, to "swallow" tiny Albania, assuming that their appetite for subjugating weaker neighbors was as keen as his own. Only Tito, among the tributary Communist chiefs, dared object to Soviet economic exploitation. In the master plan for the Communist bloc, Yugoslavia was to remain at least temporarily an underindustrialized country and a producer of raw materials. In April 1947, without asking Moscow's permission, Tito launched an ambitious five year plan of economic development.

Early in 1948 Stalin decided to discipline the unruly Yugoslavs. In February, after a stormy meeting in the Kremlin, he forced the head of their delegation to sign a humiliating promise to consult him on all future questions of foreign policy. The Yugoslav trade mission in Moscow was rudely ignored, treatment verging on a breach of commercial relations. In March, Soviet advisers and specialists were withdrawn, an act that prompted a respectful letter to Molotov inquiring about the nature of Soviet complaints. At last Stalin's resentment broke into the open. His reply (signed also by Molotov) was crude and haughty, spitefully cataloging a host of petty and ridiculous charges that had little to do with the real issues. Tito's answer, approved by the party Central Committee on April 12–13, maintained a polite tone and diplomatically assumed that Moscow's attitude was based on "insufficient knowledge" furnished by persons whose information was "inaccurate

and tendentious." The Soviet aspersions were nevertheless re-
butted with such obstinate tenacity that Stalin must have been
provoked beyond endurance. "I will shake my little finger," he
assured Khrushchev, "and there will be no more Tito."

On May 4 Stalin dispatched a letter of some four thousand
words to Belgrade. Couched in still more offensive prose, it embellished the original indictment and pronounced the Yugoslav
leaders "arrogant" and "intoxicated with their successes." The
dispute was a matter of principle, not of "verifying individual
facts," and he proposed referring it to the next session of the
Cominform.[6] Tito declined to attend or to send a representative,
and in June the Cominform delegates, meeting in Bucharest,
obediently expelled the errant Yugoslavs. Zhdanov, Stalin's deputy, engineered the verdict, offering the fatuous charge that Tito
was an "imperialist spy."

Moscow's interdict only fanned the spirit of national pride.
Tito's popularity soared to new heights, confounding Stalin's expectation that a rebellious party and a sullen populace would
make short work of the Titoist clique. Instead, Tito purged his
party of its pro-Soviet elements, although without imitating the
brutal severity characteristic of purges in the Soviet Union.

Belgrade kept up the pretense that Stalin could somehow be
dissociated from the acts of his government, and a few party members sincerely believed that Zhdanov and Molotov were the real
villains. By late 1949 the continued virulence of Soviet propaganda convinced even these innocents that Yugoslavia was not
the victim of some cosmic misunderstanding. Stalin's name ceased
to be invoked in the liturgy of Marxism-Leninism, and the party
theoreticians reluctantly concluded that Stalinism had perverted
the true faith.

The Yugoslav schism was irreversible. Stalin could not lose face
by apology or compromise; and though he tried to force Tito to
submit and recant by military threats and economic blockade,
geography and Western aid combined to save the Yugoslav apos-
tates. Fearing that the seductive appeal of Titoism might prove
contagious, Stalin directed a thorough purge of the satellite parties as a precautionary measure. The Albanian leadership, having
risen to power under Yugoslav tutelage, was particularly suspect.
Premier Enver Hoxha gained Stalin's backing, and in the spring
of 1949 he ousted the rival faction, and had its leader, Koci Xoxe,
executed for subversive contact with Tito. Later in the year spectacular public trials marked the fall of Traicho Kostov in Bulgaria and Laszlo Rajk in Hungary, both hanged for an assort-

ment of "treasonable" acts. Wladyslaw Gomulka, the Polish suzerain, was disgraced and eventually jailed. Miraculously avoiding the hangman's noose, he outlived Stalin and eventually regained his place as the party chief. Romania emerged relatively unscathed by "nationalist deviationism," while Czechoslovakia, as a latecomer to Communist ranks, escaped the more sensational forms of heresy hunting until 1952.

Tito's defection gave an unexpected assist to the Truman Doctrine. A majority of the Greek Communists sided with Stalin, and their army commander, Markos Vafiades, was lured to Bulgarian soil and arrested in August 1948 to forestall any outbreaks of Greek Titoism. Yugoslav supplies, already reduced to a trickle, ceased altogether; and in July the guerrillas were denied sanctuary as government troops, armed and equipped by the United States, forced their mountain strongholds.

Amid the welter of international incidents and political alarms that heralded the early stages of the cold war, nothing had occurred to suggest that an armed conflict might be imminent. That attitude was rudely shaken in the summer of 1948 when Stalin chose to isolate Berlin, a four power enclave in the Soviet zone, from contact with the West. The United States and its European allies had been moving toward the creation of a West German state without consulting the Soviet Union. Stalin's riposte was a drastic but not illogical means of exerting counterpressure, and for both sides Berlin symbolized their political bridgehead in Central Europe. Late in June, before the Soviet blockade had been completed, the United States began an airlift to feed and supply the population of West Berlin. There was only one encouraging aspect of the crisis: Moscow and Washington avoided a military solution. Armed convoys could have broken the blockade, and Soviet planes could have disrupted the airlift. If Stalin and Truman failed to achieve peace, at least they strove to avoid war.

In August, Stalin received Western negotiators on two occasions with benign affability, promising each time to raise the blockade in return for a gesture toward delaying the incipient West German regime. His terms were refused, and as the winter months passed with no pause in the efficiency of the airlift, Moscow's bargaining power began to seep away. In the spring Stalin conceded defeat. All restrictions were lifted, and on May 23, 1949, the Federal Republic of West Germany was established as a part of the Western bloc. So far had the wartime alliance disintegrated that the former partners now vied for Germany's favor only four years after Hitler's crushing defeat.

The partition of Germany, a convenient and presumably temporary arrangement in 1945, became the unexpected means of maintaining a new balance of power in Central Europe. Both contestants maneuvered to achieve German unity on their own terms, but it was fortunate for the future stability of Europe that Germany's population and resources remained divided. To offset the Western creation, a Soviet-sponsored German Democratic Republic was organized in the fall of 1949. A replica of the other Russian appendages, the regime was ruled by Walter Ulbricht, a trusted Stalinist who supplanted Wilhelm Pieck and assumed leadership of the Socialist Unity party in 1950.

An armaments race, latent until 1949, was given momentum with the signing in April of a twenty-year military alliance—the North Atlantic Treaty—by most of the Western nations. The United States had demobilized its army after the war, relying on a monopoly of the atomic bomb as a sufficient guarantee of European security. Soviet forces, though less drastically cut, were reduced to less than three million men from a wartime strength of nearly twelve million. The Truman Doctrine and its aftermath caused Stalin to expand his army. The implied Soviet threat to occupy western Europe in the event of an American nuclear attack provided an uneasy military stalemate. The deterrent effect of the North Atlantic Treaty seemed more vital than ever to Washington when the Soviet Union—years ahead of most Western predictions—succeeded in exploding its own nuclear device in August 1949. The Russians, too, could now indulge in "atomic diplomacy," as they had so freely accused the Americans of doing. Nevertheless the United States, by its superior stockpile of atomic weapons, its long range bombers, and its overseas air bases, retained a wide margin of superiority in case of a nuclear holocaust.

The cold war, with Europe as the matrix of the dispute, spread to East Asia in 1949, upsetting the calculations of Russians and Americans alike. The Chinese Communists, contrary to Stalin's expectations, defeated the Nationalists and drove Chiang Kai-shek into an ignominious exile on the island of Formosa. This sudden accretion of Communist power on the Asiatic mainland alarmed the United States more than the Soviet "conquest" of eastern Europe. Certainly the creation of a vast Eurasian domain officially committed to the Communist way of life was not a reality that the capitalist West could view with complacency. If Washington accepted the proposition that China had become the Far Eastern outpost of Moscow's "international Communist conspiracy," Stalin was under no delusion that Mao Tse-tung and his colleagues were his pawns on a global chessboard. Perhaps his experience with Tito taught him prudence, for he treated his new partners with circumspection.

For their part, the leaders of Red China had reason to be disdainful of Stalin's counsel: repeatedly advised to abandon their futile civil war, they had plunged ahead each time. It was thus with pride and self-confidence that they contemplated a victory won without the assistance of their strongest ally and against a regime receiving the open support of the United States. Yet they considered themselves orthodox disciples of Stalin on doctrinal matters and were content to echo Moscow's pronouncements. To Stalin, whose suspicion of popular revolution had deepened with the years, the appearance of a dynamic and powerful new China on his Asiatic doorstep was an embarrassing and not entirely welcome addition to the Communist "family of nations." But he could hardly be anything but grateful for an ally whose manpower, resources, and ideological commitment had favorably altered the world balance of power.

The Russian concessions won at China's expense during the Yalta Conference and redeemed by the Red Army's invasion of Manchuria were now subject to revision. Mao headed a large delegation to Moscow in December 1949, and his protracted stay indicated some tough-minded bargaining. The resultant Sino-Soviet Pact (February 14, 1950) included a thirty-year defensive alliance and agreements phasing out the Soviet hegemony over Manchuria. Loans and technical assistance were also provided, though Stalin was rather parsimonious until China's involvement in the Korean War.

The United States refused Peking diplomatic recognition and blocked its representation in the United Nations. Outwardly incensed by this shabby treatment, Stalin was not entirely displeased: his authority as spokesman for the Communist world remained undiminished. Moscow's moral obligation to support China was fulfilled by a Soviet boycott of the U.N. Security Council beginning in January 1950. The Russian representatives were still absent when the Korean conflict burst upon the world five months later. For the first time the uneasy truce of the cold war was shattered by bloodshed.

A Japanese colony from 1910 to 1945, Korea had been divided between Soviet and American occupation forces at the close of the Pacific War. The two countries established regimes reflecting opposing political aims: a Communist dictatorship under Premier Kim Il Sung in the North, a Right-wing dictatorship—somewhat disguised—under President Syngman Rhee in the South. Soviet and American troops withdrew in 1948–1949, leaving sizable military missions to train the two burgeoning Korean armies. Border raids and verbal provocations had become so commonplace that when the North Korean army attacked in strength on June 25, 1950, it caught the South by surprise. The Western powers pointed to Moscow as the ultimate source of aggression—certainly a reasonable assumption. But it is conceivable that the Korean Communists acted without Stalin's express permission. A forewarned Soviet delegation would normally be expected to return to the Security Council in time to veto its resolutions in support of South Korea. The Russians did not, in fact, end their boycott until August 1. Nor had Stalin previously shown any interest in sponsoring armed aggression. He had always preferred diplomatic pressure or political collusion, and during the Greek and Chinese civil wars he had been cautious to the point of timidity. If he did succumb to temptation, Washington's apparent intention of excluding Korea from its "defense perimeter" must have been the determining factor.

As the war broadened with the intervention of the United States, Stalin declined to become involved. He refused to replace the heavy equipment lost by the North Koreans and expressed interest in an Indian proposal to solve the conflict. There was no lack of rhetorical support for their Korean votaries in the United Nations, however, and the Communist press mounted its customary propaganda offensive against the West.

The Chinese decision to enter the war in the fall of 1950, following the American counter-invasion of North Korea, was presumably made after consultation with the Russians. Soviet war matériel, including new jet aircraft, sustained the Chinese "volunteer" army until a military stalemate near the original boundary had been achieved. As the first anniversary of the war approached, Moscow seized the diplomatic initiative for the first time. U.N. representative Jacob Malik's cease-fire proposal led to long and tedious negotiations punctuated by occasional skirmishes. Deadlocked on the repatriation procedure for Communist prisoners of war, the contestants settled the issue in July 1953 when Stalin had passed from the scene. His demise, by allowing a relaxation of the Communist "hard line," contributed to the successful conclusion of the armistice agreement, but a cure for the cold war by relieving the Korean symptoms was not forthcoming.

CHAPTER XI

The Death of a Tyrant

STALIN ATTAINED THE RIPE STATUS OF A SEPTUAGENARIAN IN DECEM-
ber 1949. The public veneration of Communism's secular deity
managed to surpass the ritual adulation of his previous birthday
celebrations. The party hacks, specialists in the Stalinist argot,
cranked out the same tired phrases; the international Communist
press delivered the expected encomiums; and the party leaders
monopolized a special issue of *Pravda* to convey their fulsome
praise. Birthday presents, many of them elaborate and expensive
works of art, poured in from all over the world and were donated
to a Museum of Gifts that had been opened in Moscow in 1950. A
spectacular parade on Red Square climaxed the festivities.

But no amount of unctuous flattery or ceremonial tribute
could stay the ravages of time. The dictator had grown old, and
though no one dared to say so openly, even the "great Stalin" was
only a mortal man. While there is no evidence that he became
senile—or indeed a "madman" in the conventional sense—the
physical and psychological decay of his last years was pronounced.
A Yugoslav visitor, Milovan Djilas, noticed signs of debility as
early as 1948. Stalin, he wrote, "had always enjoyed eating well."
Now he "exhibited gluttony, as though he feared that there
would not be enough of the desired food left for him. On the
other hand, he drank less and more cautiously, as though measur-
ing every drop—to avoid any ill effects." Djilas, who was something of an ascetic Communist, was taken aback by the sybaritic
flavor of the dinner he attended. "The confinement, the inanity
and senselessness of the life these Soviet leaders were living gathered about their superannuated chief" depressed him. He recalled that "Peter the Great likewise held such suppers with his
assistants at which they gorged and drank themselves into a stu-
por while ordaining the fate of Russia and the Russian people."
He felt that Stalin's intellect had also declined. In 1945 the Soviet
chieftain had been "lively, quick-witted, and had a pointed sense
of humor. . . . Now he laughed at inanities and shallow jokes.
On one occasion he not only failed to get the political point of an

anecdote I told him in which he outsmarted Churchill and Roosevelt, but I had the impression that he was offended, in the manner of old men. I perceived an awkward astonishment on the faces of the rest of the party." "In one thing, though," Djilas continued, "he was still the Stalin of old: stubborn, sharp, suspicious whenever anyone disagreed with him. He even cut Molotov, and one could feel the tension between them. Everyone paid court to him, avoiding any expression of opinion before he expressed his, and then hastening to agree with him." [1]

There are indications that Stalin's condition grew steadily worse, though the testimony of an independent observer such as Djilas is lacking. In a moment of anger, he even accused his daughter of making anti-Soviet statements. On another occasion, when Svetlana asked why her aunts had been arrested, he explained vaguely: "They talked a lot. They knew too much and they talked too much. And it helped our enemies." He had erected his own delusional system, and it had become so obvious that Svetlana could recognize the symptoms—though perhaps not at the time—as a full fledged persecution mania. It is highly unlikely, however, that his mental state was "all a result of being lonely and desolate." [2] Erratic behavior, morbid suspiciousness, and a conspiratorial view of external reality—personality traits perceptible from the 1930's onward—point to a serious disorder which, in the absence of more accurate information, can only be diagnosed as paranoia. Progressive arteriosclerosis furnished the physiological basis, but Stalin's pathology seems to have been partly psychic in origin. Psychosomatic medicine, still in its infancy, can provide little insight into his case without adequate supporting data.

The *Vozhd* made no move to groom a successor or to prepare his disciples for his inevitable demise. Like many aging men, especially those who have acquired status and power, he was psychologically unprepared to accept retirement or the certainty of incapacity or death. He probably assumed, despite the steady impairment of his health, that he was destined to live a good deal longer. Georgians, of all the nationalities of the Soviet Union, were noted for their longevity, and Stalin had access to the best in medical service though he apparently failed to avail himself of it. He did make one concession to his deteriorating health: he gave up smoking. This was no mean achievement—in fact a triumph of self-discipline—for a man who had been an inveterate pipe and cigarette smoker for more than half a century.

Stalin's last extended journey from Moscow was a visit to his homeland in the summer and fall of 1951. He vacationed at Li-kani "Palace," an old hunting lodge overlooking a gorge of the Kura River at Borzhomi, Georgia, and he recalled with barely concealed nostalgia a previous visit in 1922 with his young wife. Contrary to his usual custom, he allowed news of his trip to enter the public domain and had been overwhelmed by an idolatrous crowd gathered to greet him at the Kutais railway station. This spontaneous outpouring of sentiment for a native son contrasted sharply with the mechanical homage of his official appearances. But displays of emotion—always excepting his own—irritated him, and after his unpleasant experience at Kutais he made only one attempt to leave the seclusion of Borzhomi. Intending per-haps to renew the familiar scenes of his youth in Tbilisi and Gori, he set off on the road to Bakuriani without an elaborate retinue. He never got past the first village. Carpets were spread on the road, and the local residents swarmed around his car and in-sisted that he join them for a banquet. One's imagination boggles at the improbability of the event: the all powerful dictator, testy and embarrassed, virtually shanghaied by simple Georgian vil-lagers. Discouraged from further sightseeing, he returned to his retreat at Borzhomi—a hostage to his own fame.

Stalin's only unfulfilled ambition, we may speculate with rea-sonable assurance, was an intellectual stature equivalent to that of Marx and Lenin. True, he was daily reminded by the printed word that he had indeed attained that lofty eminence: the sacred trinity, "Marx-Lenin-Stalin," had become a tedious and almost mandatory refrain for speakers, journalists, and scholars. Yet there was no substantial body of theoretical work from which eager practitioners of *tsitatnichestvo*—citation-mongering—could draw. Even Stalin, whose capacity for self-deception was nearly inexhaustible, must have recognized his deficiency. Having deliv-ered his *ex cathedra* judgment on the esoteric subject of linguis-tics in 1950, he turned to a more appropriate topic for a Marxist —economic theory.

Published in October 1952, Stalin's "Economic Problems of So-cialism in the U.S.S.R." had been generated by a previous discus-sion among academicians on the preparation of a textbook in po-litical economy. The lengthy essay, though a mediocre and pe-dantic exercise in Marxist scholasticism, dealt forthrightly with the vexing question of capitalist stability. Not surprisingly, for Varga's reprimand had indicated the trend of Stalin's thought, he clung to Marxist fundamentals: the "disintegration of a single, universal world market"—the most important economic consequence of World War II—had aggravated the "general crisis in the world capitalist system." He foresaw a clash among the "imperialists" rather than a concerted assault on the "camp of socialism." In denying the likelihood of an immediate or even an ultimate conflict involving the Soviet Union, he delivered a mild rebuke to the proponents of a more aggressive foreign policy.

If Stalin was now signaling the shift to a defensive strategy of caution and conservatism, he went out of his way to demonstrate a vigilant regard for the national interest. The incident involved the recall of the American ambassador, George F. Kennan, whose reputation as the brains behind Washington's "containment" policy could not have made him a Kremlin favorite. Convinced that Stalin's "hard" line would inevitably mellow, Kennan was given a cool reception in his attempts to initiate exploratory talks with Soviet officials. In September 1952, on a trip to western Europe, he dropped an incautious remark to reporters comparing the political atmosphere in Moscow to that in Berlin during the war. The Soviet press was stung to an angry retort, and the Foreign Office seized upon the ambassador's indiscretion by declaring him *persona non grata* in a note to Washington.

Stalin's timing was masterly. His essay appeared on October 2, Kennan's recall came the next day, and on the fifth the Nineteenth Party Congress convened in Moscow. As the first such gathering since March 1939—Stalin had simply ignored the party statutes requiring a congress at least once every three years—it was a momentous occasion. The "genius-leader and teacher of all progressive mankind" was then approaching his seventy-third year, and the world press anticipated, if not major policy decisions, some portents of the political succession. Malenkov delivered the keynote address—the report of the Central Committee —a privilege that Stalin had not relinquished for almost thirty years. Since the "Economic Problems" had been deliberately released on the eve of the congress, the delegates were transformed into a dutiful claque for the purpose of paying tribute to Stalin's intellectual genius.

Malenkov, while installed as the favorite, could scarcely conclude that his chief was preparing a graceful exit. The problem of succession was confused by replacing the Politburo and Orgburo with an unwieldy new body—the Presidium—containing twenty-five members and eleven alternates. In addition, the five-man party Secretariat was doubled in size. Then considered a means of infusing the party leadership with new blood, the reorganization was given a more sinister interpretation by Khrushchev in 1956:

Stalin "aimed at the removal of the old Political Bureau and the bringing in of less experienced persons so that these would extol him in all sorts of ways." [3]

Stalin sat silent and inscrutable throughout the proceedings. At the final session he closed the congress with a brief inspirational message tailored especially for the large delegation of foreign Communists. These innocuous remarks, interrupted by frequent ceremonial applause, concluded with the customary "stormy, unabating applause, turning into an ovation" that marked the dictator's formal speeches. It was to be his valedictory address.

During the winter of 1952–1953 Stalin's mental condition deteriorated still further. "He trusted no one," said Khrushchev, "and none of us could trust him. He would not let us do the work he was no longer capable of. It was very difficult for us." [4] Suffering from delusions of persecution—a classic case of psychological projection—he could react in the only way he knew: by crushing his "enemies." Conspirators were everywhere, it seemed, and because of his distrust of the usual political channels he relied increasingly on the elaborate personal apparatus built up over the years by his loyal factotum Poskrebyshev, the "Soviet Rasputin." Stalin's anti-Semitism having crystalized, Jews—as such, and not simply as "Zionists" or "rootless cosmopolitans"—were drawn into his nightmare world of political conspiracy. A trial run had been arranged in Czechoslovakia, where an estimated eighty per cent of those arrested during the party purge of 1951–1952 were Jews. Rudolf Slansky, the former party chief, was among them. In November 1952 he and thirteen other prominent Communists, of whom eleven were Jews, went on trial in Prague. The fantastic assortment of charges included Titoism, Trotskyism, Zionism, and espionage for the United States. The prosecution stressed the Jewish names of the majority and linked them to "international Jewry." All pleaded guilty and eleven defendants, including Slansky, were executed.

The Soviet press featured the news from Prague, emphasizing the "American Zionist" aspects of the "plot." Anti-Zionist propaganda and the arrest or disgrace of highly placed Jews, none of them deemed important enough for a repetition of the Slansky trial, continued in Communist Europe. However, no blanket edict against Jews in positions of political trust was forthcoming from Moscow, and a number of highly placed Jews—Premier Mathias Rakosi of Hungary was an outstanding example—enjoyed every evidence of the Kremlin's favor.

Among the Soviet elite the atmosphere became suffused with fear and anxiety as the press called for "vigilance" and a tightening of party discipline. A purge of Ukrainian officials resulted in the death penalty for several Jews accused of "counter-revolutionary wrecking." Cases of laxity, nepotism, speculation, embezzlement, and espionage became commonplace during the winter months. But none had the sensational impact of the "Doctors' Plot," a macabre affair first revealed to the public on January 13, 1953. A "terrorist group" of nine Kremlin physicians, most of them Jewish, were charged with murdering through deliberate malpractice former Politburo members Alexander Shcherbakov in 1945 and Andrei Zhdanov in 1948. Allegedly these "monsters in human form" had also conspired unsuccessfully to kill a number of military commanders, and most of them were said to have been agents for American intelligence in conjunction with the Jewish Joint Distribution Committee, a charitable organization based in the United States. With its anti-Semitic overtones and analogies to the Great Purge, the "conspiracy" bore all the earmarks of a Stalinist fabrication. Aside from the old Politburo as his ultimate target, Stalin struck more directly at Beria: the carelessness of the state security service, the press implied, had permitted the nefarious doctors to practice undetected for many years.

Stalin carried out the investigation without consulting the newly chosen Presidium. He reportedly gave the minister of state security, Semyon Ignatiev, an ultimatum: "If you do not obtain confessions from the doctors we will shorten you by a head." "Stalin personally called the investigative judge," Khrushchev later maintained, "gave him instructions, advised him on which investigative methods should be used; these methods were simple— beat, beat and, once again, beat." When the required confessions had been extracted, Stalin presented them to his skeptical assistants—now hardly more than flunkies—as a *fait accompli*. "You are blind like young kittens," he told them. "What will happen without me? The country will perish because you do not know how to recognize enemies." [5]

Stalin received several foreign visitors in February, and they described him as amiable and seemingly in good health. The Indian ambassador, K.P.S. Menon, conversed with him at length on the seventeenth. For the most part they spoke on nonpolitical topics, and Stalin, falling into an old habit, doodled on a pad of paper. Out of context, he remarked: "The peasant is a very simple man but a very wise man. When the wolf attacks him, he does not attempt to teach it morals, but tries to kill it. And the wolf knows this and behaves accordingly." [6] Menon then noticed that the doodles were wolves in various postures. Stalin did not identify the "wolves," but it was obvious that another bloodbath to rival that of the thirties was in the preliminary stages.

Late in February the "vigilance" campaign in the press ceased rather abruptly. Stalin's role in this mysterious shift in the party line is unknown. He was not ill, for on Saturday night, February 28, he invited his closest associates to dinner at Kuntsevo, and the old man was in rare good humor. "On Sundays," Khrushchev afterward related, "Stalin usually telephoned each of us to discuss business, but that Sunday he did not call, which struck us as odd. He did not come back to town on Monday [March 2], and on Monday evening the head of his bodyguard called us and said Stalin was ill." He had been stricken with a cerebral hemorrhage sometime during the night and was found at three A.M. lying on a rug by the sofa. Why the party leaders were not notified sooner has not been explained.

Stalin lay in a coma, speechless and the right side of his body paralyzed. Although he was beyond medical help, a frantic team of doctors and nurses—his regular physician, Vladimir Vinogradov, was still under arrest—busied themselves with leeches, cardiograms, and X-rays in a vain attempt to revive him. Nearly all the members of the old Politburo were present. Stalin briefly regained consciousness and, according to Khrushchev, "He shook us by the hand and tried to joke with us, smiling feebly and waving with his good arm to a picture over his bed of a baby lamb being fed with a spoon by a little girl. Now, he indicated by gestures, he was just as helpless as the baby lamb." [7] A strong heart beat sustained life while the hemorrhaging gradually spread to the unaffected portions of his brain. He expired on the evening of March 5, his last hours an agonizing struggle against slow suffocation. Most of his former colleagues were in tears, torn by the contradictory emotions of "sorrow and relief." [8] "After all," said Khrushchev, "we were his pupils and owed him everything. Like Peter the Great, Stalin fought barbarism with barbarism but he was a great man." Only Beria behaved in an unseemly manner, barely concealing his lust for power now that his mentor was dead.

The delay in informing the public—the first announcement of

Stalin's illness was withheld until March 4—contributed to a suspicion that his death was not entirely due to natural causes. But the rumors sprang mainly from the premise that coincidence has its limits—that the tyrant's death came at so opportune a moment for his successors that they must have hastened him toward his end. One version, "the most generally accepted in the best-informed Soviet circles," has it that the fatal stroke was brought on when Kaganovich—or Voroshilov in other accounts—tore up his party card and threw it in Stalin's face when the latter revealed his plans to deport all Jews to Siberia.[9] Another version embellishes the card-tearing incident by claiming an accidental fall: the semi-conscious Stalin was revived and ultimately murdered with poisoned brandy administered by Molotov.[10] Other fanciful variations assure a firm place in popular mythology for the circumstances of Stalin's death.

The public obsequies were observed with appropriate tributes to the mighty leader who had fallen. Yet the eulogies of his chief heirs were almost perfunctory compared to the repellent flattery they had contrived during his lifetime. The attitude of the general public was difficult to gauge, but it seemed to register more shock and awe than genuine grief. If a sense of national bereavement, so noticeable in Lenin's passing, was absent, the assumption of Western commentators that the Russian people were glad to be rid of the aged despot was wide of the mark. To millions of the unsophisticated, unable or unwilling to delve beneath the political façade, Stalin died as he had lived—an effective creation of the Kremlin's propaganda apparatus. The average citizen, even when alerted by a sense of personal grievance against the regime, could have little knowledge of the scope of his misdeeds. He was the Communist Tsar, and like the monarchs of old Russia, he was mourned by his dutiful subjects.

Stalin's body lay in state for three days in the Hall of Columns of Moscow's House of Unions building, once an ornate club for the Tsarist nobility. Tens of thousands waited in the cold for a glimpse of the embalmed corpse. At nearby Trubnaya Square the impatient crowds, wedged between the buildings and a row of army trucks, stampeded. Scores were trampled to death or maimed before order could be restored. This grotesque human sacrifice furnished an ironic epitaph to the savagery of the Stalin era.

The funeral rites were held on the morning of March 9 in Red Square, and the pallbearers—Malenkov, Beria, Molotov,

Khrushchev, Bulganin, Voroshilov, Kaganovich, and Mikoyan—constituted a ruling oligarchy of eight. A ninth figure was added for ceremonial purposes: Vasily Stalin, the dictator's surviving son. Khrushchev, Malenkov, Beria, and Molotov spoke briefly in conventional terms, and only the last seemed genuinely moved by the great man's passing. Burial took place in the Lenin mausoleum before the great Kremlin wall, the highest honor the party could bestow. Thirty rifle volleys were fired in salute, the Kremlin chimes rang out, and three minutes of silent respect was observed throughout the Soviet Union as steam whistles blew a final tribute. The funeral was over: the era of Stalin had ended. But his successors discovered that while the flesh is mortal the spirit lives on. Stalin's ghost was to present unexpected problems of exorcism.

CHAPTER XII

Legend and Legacy

THE STALINIST EPIGONI ACTED WITH ALMOST INDECENT HASTE TO consolidate their rule. But without the master at the helm they seemed to lack self-confidence: the "collective leadership," announcing the redisposition of the top party and government posts on March 7, called for "unity" and the "prevention of any kind of disorder and panic." It was as if they feared that the population, docile under Stalin, might rise up against those who would maintain authority in his name.

Careful at first to invoke the symbols of Stalinism, the oligarchs (headed by Malenkov as premier and first among equals) grew bolder and within weeks had begun a partial dismantling of the elaborate police state apparatus that seemed a permanent fixture of the regime. A limited amnesty for political prisoners led in time to a drastic reduction of the labor camp population, and the promise of a new code of criminal justice offered hope of a decisive break with the Stalinist heritage. The "doctors' plot" was exposed as a criminal fraud and its victims rehabilitated. The anti-Semitic insinuations in the press had already ceased, though the party did not lift various unofficial measures of discrimination against Jews. Foreign policy also shared in the post-Stalin "thaw." An unwonted diplomatic courtesy softened the Kremlin's "hard line," and even the surly Molotov, who had resumed his old post of foreign minister, reappeared as an apostle of international conciliation. Unfortunately, American diplomacy had congealed in a rigid anti-Communist mold, and the Korean settlement scarcely altered the deep-seated antagonism between Washington and Moscow.

The overweening Beria was eliminated from the Presidium in the summer of 1953 and subsequently executed. His downfall marked an end to the autonomous domain of the secret police which Yagoda, Yezhov, and Beria had spawned under Stalin's beneficent patronage. He later became a convenient scapegoat for a number of Stalin's blunders. The remaining party leaders, still insecure but gaining in experience and self-assurance, disagreed on how to confront the formidable Stalinist legend. Few if any wished to preserve the system intact, nor did the consensus that emerged in favor of moderate reform appear to include any fervent anti-Stalinists. Yet the pressures within the party and within the new Soviet elite for a repudiation of the "cult of personality" were building up. De-Stalinization acquired momentum while remaining unobtrusive. The hallowed name, which the press had used with such profuse monotony, had ceased to appear as a regular feature of Communist litany as early as April 1953. No one ventured to attack the man and the ruler, but there were oblique forays against his ideological position, and the adulation so lavishly bestowed during his lifetime was notably absent. On special occasions—the anniversaries of Stalin's birth and death—articles commemorating his achievements appeared in the press. Even the most laudatory, however, tended to subordinate the individual to the party. To the average citizen, unskilled in the nuances of politics, his reputation remained unsullied and his place in the pantheon of Soviet heroes second only to Lenin's.

In February 1955 Khrushchev, as first secretary of the party, emerged as the top Soviet leader, and Bulganin replaced Malenkov as premier. Khrushchev's reputation as the former "Stalin of the Ukraine" and Malenkov's record as a champion of the consumer and a circumspect protagonist of "socialist legality" aroused concern abroad—and not a little in the Soviet Union—about a return to Stalinism. These fears not only proved unfounded, but the pudgy new Soviet ruler became as outspoken an opponent of the late dictator as the most vociferous anti-Communist in the Western world.

Khrushchev delivered his anti-Stalinist bombshell at a secret session of the Twentieth Party Congress in February 1956. Contrary to the opinion then prevalent that his rambling four hour speech cataloging Stalin's crimes and follies was an impromptu performance, it had a lengthy gestation period. A quiet and thorough investigation had uncovered much that even the party chieftains, presumably hardened by their years of service as Stalin's toadies, could not stomach. Having elevated Khrushchev to the number one spot in the party pyramid—he had not seized power in Stalin's fashion—the junta bore a collective responsibility for the precipitate course of de-Stalinization. Yet Khrushchev was not simply a mouthpiece for his colleagues. He had a quality of stubborn tenacity, and there is a grain of truth in the Soviet writer Ilya Ehrenburg's otherwise mistaken contention that "only an ignorant man like Khrushchev" could have made the speech:

"A more sophisticated man would never have dared."[1] If the party Presidium had been composed of intellectuals rather than tough-minded politicians, perhaps the consequences would have been more readily foreseen and more discreet anti-Stalinist methods pursued.

Although shock tactics were used for the general public, the Communist elite—both foreign and domestic—was given some forewarning. As early as June 1955, upon returning from delivering a belated but handsome apology to President Tito for the unpleasantries of 1948, Khrushchev stopped off in Sofia and pretested some of his later charges before an audience of Bulgarian party leaders.[2] In January 1956, a month before the party congress, Communist delegates from abroad were briefed in Moscow about the forthcoming attack on Stalin. But the briefing sessions were not entirely candid about the extent of the onslaught—possibly they could not have been, without access to Khrushchev's text—and in any case the rank and file were left in ignorance.

Prior to Khrushchev's dramatic revelations, Mikoyan offered the first open criticism of Stalin in almost thirty years. He virtually repudiated the "Economic Problems of Socialism in the U.S.S.R." and derided the notorious "Short Course" on the history of the party which had for so many years epitomized the degradation of Stalinist "scholarship." Other speakers condemned aspects of Stalin's policy without mentioning him by name. The party had chipped away at the Stalin cult with alacrity, and the real task of demolition was left to its first secretary. Khrushchev discarded the inhibitions of his predecessors and mounted a frontal assault so devastating that a major rehabilitation of Stalin's reputation in the immediate future became politically untenable. In its specific details the indictment was more grisly than the most hostile anti-Stalinist biographies published abroad. And its references to the dictator's mental instability went beyond any information previously available. But for all its scathing iconoclasm the speech stayed scrupulously within the framework of Communist tradition: Stalin's most heinous crime had been his decimation of the party (and to a lesser extent the Red Army). The broader spectrum of his terror—the peasants who perished in the collectivization drive, the "traitors" eliminated during the Moscow trials, and the anonymous millions who suffered from Stalin's "justice" during the Great Purge and beyond —were ignored in the carefully selected documentation. Stalinism, it seemed, was but an aberration of history whose occurrence bore no relationship to the Bolshevik heritage or to the Soviet political system. Nor did Khrushchev implicate himself in his master's crimes, though the record indicates that he was as deeply involved in the purges as any of his associates. He emerged—largely by innuendo—as a courageous and principled Bolshevik who had stood up to the Boss when necessity demanded, while his comrades, especially Malenkov, were tarnished with the brush of expediency—or worse. In all, it was a skillful production and added moral stature to Khrushchev's growing but still uncertain political authority.

The text of the speech was never published in the Soviet Union. Party members received oral summaries, often quite explicit, but even these muted versions were strong medicine to the millions of believers left floundering in a state of shock and consternation. Although Georgia was treated as a special case—only rumors of the Khrushchev speech percolated in—the impact of this rude desanctification elsewhere in the Soviet Union could not be concealed. Eventually there were student riots at Tbilisi State University protesting this supreme indignity to the memory of a national hero, and throughout the Georgian Republic memorial meetings honored the third anniversary of Stalin's death. The substance of the new anti-Stalinist dispensation eventually filtered down to the masses, whose stolid receptivity proved equal once more to this latest sensation from Moscow.

The non-Communist world learned of the speech in June 1953 when the United States Department of State obtained the text from a confidential source in eastern Europe and released it to the press. The Communist parties of the West, with no premonitory hints, were thrown into paroxysms of doubt and confusion. But it was chiefly the intellectuals who agonized while the solid core of followers, inured to the changing winds from the Kremlin, submitted to party discipline. Palmiro Togliatti, the Italian party chief, delivered an extensive critique of the Soviet regime unprecedented in the annals of international Communism. "All that was good was attributed to the superhuman, positive qualities of one man," he declared. "Now all that is evil is attributed to his equally exceptional and even astonishing faults. . . . The true problems are evaded, which are why and how Soviet society could and did reach certain forms alien to the democratic way and to the legality which it had set for itself, even to the point of degeneration." [3] That he was neither censured nor excommunicated was in itself a remarkable commentary on the changing political climate in Moscow.

The Soviet satellites were the most deeply affected by de-Stalinization. Unknowingly, and with an ingenuousness that bordered on the foolhardy for a seasoned politician Khrushchev had opened a Pandora's box. The Communist appendages became restive, then rebellious, and the Kremlin's new rulers learned by experience what the old autocrat had known instinctively: that reform combined with weakness and hesitation can be more explosive revolutionary ingredients than poverty and oppression.

The Poles were far in the vanguard as the "peoples' democracies" stepped up the pace of liberalization in the wake of Khrushchev's startling exposé. Wladyslaw Gomulka, whose credentials as a living martyr to Stalinist persecution were unsurpassed among Polish Communists, regained the party leadership in October 1956 after outmaneuvering a formidable Soviet delegation that Khrushchev himself led to Warsaw. He contrived his own brand of national Communism, a feat that the Hungarian party failed to duplicate as a popular revolution in Budapest threatened a complete break with Moscow. Imre Nagy, the "Hungarian Gomulka," was swept aside as the Kremlin resorted to brute force in the worst tradition of Stalin. Soviet intervention successfully crushed the "freedom fighters" but conferred a new legacy of bitterness upon the global struggle. Khrushchev's own political future was jeopardized, and in self-defense he was obliged to conduct a partial retreat along the Stalinist terrain he had traversed so insouciantly earlier in the year.

That Khrushchev would not only manage to salvage his career but emerge as the sole major survivor of the ten-man Presidium seemed less than likely in the closing weeks of 1956. He appeased the Stalinists by praising the dictator as a "great Marxist" and "fighter against imperialism." "The imperialists call us Stalinists," he declared. "Well, when it comes to fighting imperialists, we are all Stalinists." [4] Since the Chinese Communists had emerged as neo-Stalinists, Khrushchev chose the occasion of a Kremlin reception for Foreign Minister Chou En-lai in January 1957 to offer further homage: for those who had devoted their lives to the revolutionary struggle "Stalin's name was inseparable from Marxism-Leninism." Molotov and Kaganovich, the two leading Stalinists, had meanwhile been restored to favor after a demotion during the previous summer.

In June 1957 the Stalinists and "liberals" of the Presidium combined against Khrushchev. Only by an adroit appeal to intraparty democracy—the first such successful maneuver since the mid-twenties—did he avoid political oblivion. A plenary session of the Central Committee upheld him, and his enemies were relegated to minor positions in the hinterlands. The political infight-ing, if no less savage than in Stalin's time, was now at least blood-less.

The triumphant Khrushchev skated a thin line between "revi-sionism" (Titoism) and "conservatism" (Stalinism). But his effort to pose as a "centrist" eventually became embroiled in the growing Sino-Soviet conflict. The Chinese adopted Stalin as an ideological talisman, not because they had revered him in the flesh but because they were confronted with the problem of "primitive socialist accumulation" that he had solved at so great a cost to the moral and intellectual fabric of Communism. They regarded the power and prosperity of the Soviet Union with envy, but it had been gained in their view at the expense of doctrinal flabbiness and a failure of nerve that permitted truckling to the "imperialists" and a loss of revolutionary zeal.

By 1961 the Aesopian language of the Russians in denouncing their Chinese brethren as "leftists," "dogmatists," and "sectar-ians" had to be discarded. The two Communist giants clashed publicly in October during the Twenty-Second Party Congress in Moscow. When Khrushchev attacked Albania, China's diminu-tive Balkan partner, for Stalinist tactics, Chou En-lai, one of the "fraternal" delegates, replied testily and left the congress in mid-session. The party leaders prescribed another round of de-Stalini-zation, this time without the secrecy that had surrounded the ini-tial assault in 1956. Again they flogged the dead horses consigned to the political glue factory—Molotov, Malenkov, Kaganovich, Voroshilov, and others. The Anti-Party Group—Khrushchev's label—was implicated in Stalin's crimes, and a number of speak-ers documented the charge with compromising tidbits drawn from the record of the Great Purge. The congress passed a resolu-tion proposing that Stalin's coffin be removed from the mauso-leum: "To leave it there would be blasphemy." An elderly female delegate was greeted with "stormy prolonged applause" when she declared, "Yesterday I asked Ilyich [Lenin] for advice, and it was as if he stood before me alive and said: 'I do not like being next to Stalin, who inflicted so much harm on the party.' " [5] That eve-ning workmen removed the embalmed corpse from its place of honor and buried it in a modest plot near the Kremlin wall. Not even a bust of the decanonized leader graced the site, a tribute that embellished the other graves in the immediate vicinity. A pointed rebuke to the Chinese Communists was concealed in the indignities to which Stalin's image—and now his corpse—was subjected. Before his departure for Peking, Chou had rendered homage at the mausoleum, depositing a floral wreath inscribed "To J. V. Stalin, the great Marxist-Leninist."

Meanwhile the material remnants of Stalinolatry had all but disappeared. The portraits, busts, and statues had been withdrawn or demolished, and the schools, factories, towns, and geographical features bearing his name had found more appropriate designations. But the ultimate humiliation came with the renaming of Stalin's city on the Volga: Stalingrad, hallowed by the deeds of the Red Army, became Volgograd. Only three major specimens of iconography survived the 1961 "purge." All were located in Gori, the dictator's Georgian birthplace: a huge statue, typically Stalinist in its tastelessness, dominating the main street; the cottage, suitably protected by an elaborate marble façade, where Stalin was born; and an ornate museum, closed to the public for several years, which reopened in 1966 with the mementoes of his long career preserved with respectful piety.

As if mesmerized by the Stalinist legend, Khrushchev could not forebear another favorable mention of the late dictator in the spring of 1962 when the political pendulum had completed its cycle and swung back in the other direction. Despite his "abuses of power," said Khrushchev, "does anyone doubt that Stalin was a Communist, that he was dedicated to Communism? If there is such a person, he must be quite without understanding. Stalin was dedicated to Communism with his whole being; everything he did was for Communism." [6] But the "general line" did not follow this tentative revaluation, and the few minor oscillations toward Stalinism in the remaining years of the Khrushchev era did not alter the basic pattern of cautious denigration.

By the late sixties the Stalinist legacy had almost imperceptibly passed from the realm of politics to that of history. Khrushchev's ouster from power in 1964 brought little change in the extreme reticence that had begun to shroud Soviet references to the details of Stalin's rule. It was almost as if his twenty-five year reign had been cast into the memory hole once reserved for his political enemies. His achievements were ascribed to the party, and the sordid features of his regime tended to be ignored or minimized. The official party history, though a vast improvement over the Stalinist textbook, shied away from a fundamental reassessment of the man and his epoch. And the rehabilitation of the lesser victims of Stalin's terror obliquely raised nagging questions about the Moscow trial defendants—and of Trotsky himself—which were answered with stubborn silence. Obliged to destroy the cult of Stalin, the party simply refurbished the venerable cult of

Lenin and gave it new status: the founder of Bolshevism now reigned supreme in the Soviet Valhalla.

The new leadership of Alexei Kosygin and Leonid Brezhnev was anxious to forget that the Stalin problem still existed. The provocation furnished by the defection of Stalin's daughter to the United States and the publication of her memoirs—an ironic footnote to the cold war—caused them only momentary embarrassment. Under their guidance the Soviet government completed the transition from barbaric despotism to a kind of constitutional oligarchy, giving promise of a flexibility that would meet the needs of an industrialized and pluralist society. But until a political elite emerged that was morally uncontaminated by Stalin's atrocities even a revival of party democracy seemed unlikely. Nor did the development of political and intellectual freedom in the Western sense appear any closer to realization as the nation celebrated the fiftieth anniversary of the Bolshevik Revolution.

The new generation of Soviet youth knew Stalin only by hearsay and by the bland and guarded references permitted by the party ideologists. His place in popular legend is assured, however, for his impact on Russian society was greater even than Lenin's. In the duration of his hegemony, the number of his subjects, and the unrestrained exercise of his power, he must be accounted the mightiest ruler in history. The Genghis Khan of revolutionary despots, he was able, like most politicians, to rationalize his crimes and follies as the inevitable price of national greatness and social progress. And unlike the bankrupt fascist dictators, he emerged from the bloody agony of World War II with the stature —however undeserved—of a world statesman.

If future historians memorialize the great tyrant as Stalin the Terrible, they will also chronicle his deeds with greater detachment than his contemporaries. Russian nationalists, whether monarchist émigrés or Soviet Marxists, can take pride in the powerful state he wrought from an unpromising heritage of military weakness, economic backwardness, and mass illiteracy. It has been argued that democratic capitalism could have accomplished as much as totalitarian Communism in achieving industrial greatness—and without the political savagery and cultural sterility that disfigured the Soviet "experiment." But such a proposition begs the question, for it assumes a social structure that did not exist in 1917: a large and enlightened middle class, a prosperous and efficient peasantry, and a skilled but docile industrial proletariat. A Westernized intellectual at the head of the party—a

Trotsky, a Zinoviev, or a Bukharin—would never have contemplated the wild excesses of a Stalin. Nor would they have stumbled into the blunder of forced "de-kulakization" or stubbornly pursued the disastrous Comintern line on German fascism in the early thirties. In the nomenclature of early Russian Social Democracy, they were the Bolshevik "softs" who would have recoiled from a brutal assault on the social and cultural heritage of the nation. Stalin, on the contrary, was an unflinching "hard" whose usefulness Lenin, almost alone, had been quick to perceive and whose coarse ruthlessness and indomitable will forged a new society in his own image.

Stalinism, although a bizarre compound of Slavophilism and Bolshevism, was not a phenomenon entirely alien to the Western tradition. Like fascism, whose roots were more obviously traceable to the pathology of industrial capitalism, Stalin's distorted version of a socialist society sought to imitate the features he most admired in the great powers of the West: their superior technology, their material affluence, and their national pride. Stalin sought short cuts to end the Slavic inferiority complex, just as Mao's Communism, with a dogmatism that seemed quite irrational to Westerners, provided a Chinese solution to a legacy of peasant slothfulness and colonial subservience.

To dismiss Stalin as a monster of tyranny—a loathsome sadist run amuck—may be morally satisfying but an exercise in futility if one seeks insight into the man or his regime. His emergence as Russia's greatest despot was no historical accident, as the Soviet leaders, contrary to their Marxist creed, would have us believe. Neither was he an "inevitable" result of the elitist party that Lenin so painstakingly constructed. It is true nonetheless that the Bolsheviks, who had the audacity and the power to overthrow the Provisional Government—that hapless symbol of Western parliamentarianism—were Marxists of a special breed. The natural selection of political struggle forced out the weak and the ineffectual in favor of the strong and the purposeful. As the Kerensky government collapsed before the Leninist onslaught, so the revolutionary romantics of Bolshevism gave way to the doctrinaire technocracy of the Stalinists. The dictator himself represented the survival of the fittest. But even he, while outwardly unperturbed by the perpetual crises of the 1920's, succumbed all too soon to the emotional hazards of personal tragedy and unlicensed power. Almost by definition a dictator cannot be a "normal" individual, and it speaks well of Stalin's native ability that his growing paranoia did not render him unfit to carry on the enormous burdens of government. A sicker man would have been overthrown by his associates, although the Russian tradition of autocracy and the centralist credo of Bolshevism inhibited both the masses and the party leadership from a concerted attack upon a well entrenched and determined ruler.

Stalin's legacy was not confined to the Soviet Union. Ironically, his one great ideological success—Mao's China—was the very area in which his limitations as strategist and seer had been so nakedly exposed. But even in China neo-Stalinism seemed unlikely to outlast the "old guard" of Maoists. The continued fragmentation of international Communism furnished the surest guarantee against a resurgence of Stalinist tendencies. The monolithic political and doctrinal hegemony that Stalin's Russia enjoyed until 1948 is beyond recall. "Liberal" Communism, contrary to the fears of the Soviet party bosses, does not lead inevitably to the uncharted perils of democratic socialism. Yet a return to the ideals of classical Marxism—to which even Stalin gave lip service—makes an increasingly strong appeal to the younger generation of the Soviet intelligentsia.

It tends to be forgotten that Marxism was not only a product of Western civilization and a searing indictment of industrial capitalism but a social philosophy that spoke with eloquence in the name of oppressed humanity. The Bolshevik variant of Marxism, though it struck roots in an environment rather different than Marx had envisaged, also proclaimed its devotion to the downtrodden masses. Its early practitioners, however misguided they may have been, were dedicated to an idea that transcended the routine political concerns of personal power and national aggrandizement. Stalin, with his shrewd practicality and stunted moral sensibilities, never relinquished the absurd notion that his system had merely brought Marxism to its logical fruition. Almost single-handedly he corrupted the ethical foundations of Communism, offering instead a mélange of political despotism and material progress that was not unattractive to millions of Soviet citizens. Nor were the dispossessed of other lands, insofar as they understood a sophisticated doctrine such as Communism, repelled by those ugly features that were widely publicized in the democratic and prosperous West. The gulf between "advanced" and "underdeveloped" nations has already become more significant than the obsolete distinction between those that are democratic and those that are Communist—the "free" and the "slave" in the antiquated parlance of the cold war.

Despite an overly rigid ideology and an ossified political structure, the Soviet Union has more in common with the industrialized "bourgeois" countries than with its Communist cousins. But the Stalinist legacy remains very much alive. A repudiation of the man is not sufficient to reform the system, and a return to Bolshevism's original heritage—Marxist social democracy—should be the essential task of the Soviet future. The auguries, though presently discouraging, are not unfavorable.

Reference Notes

CHAPTER I

1. J. V. Stalin, *Works* (Moscow, 1952–55), XII, 146.
2. Svetlana Alliluyeva, *Twenty Letters to a Friend* (New York, 1967), p. 210.
3. Joseph E. Davies, *Mission to Moscow* (New York, 1941), p. 357.
4. Walter Bedell Smith, *My Three Years in Moscow* (Philadelphia, 1949), p. 48.
5. Alliluyeva, *Twenty Letters*, p. 126.

CHAPTER II

1. A. S. Alliluyeva, *Vospominania* [Reminiscences] (Moscow, 1946), p. 167.
2. Stalin, *Works*, I, 415.
3. *Iskra*, No. 6, July 1901, quoted in L. Beria, *On the History of the Bolshevik Organizations in Transcaucasia* (Moscow, 1949), p. 34.
4. G. F. Alexandrov and others, *Joseph Stalin: A Short Biography* (Moscow, 1950), p. 18.
5. Joseph Iremaschwili [Iremashvili], *Stalin und die Tragödie Georgiens* (Berlin, 1932), p. 40.
6. Alliluyeva, *Twenty Letters*, p. 101.
7. *New York Times*, February 19, 1967.
8. Stalin, *Works*, VI, 56.
9. *Ibid.*, p. 58.
10. *Ibid.*, II, 51–52.
11. *Ibid.*, VIII, 183.
12. J. Bernard Hutton, *Stalin—The Miraculous Georgian* (London, 1961), pp. 38–40.
13. See Isaac Don Levine, *Stalin's Great Secret* (New York, 1956), and Edward Ellis Smith, *The Young Stalin* (New York, 1967).

CHAPTER III

1. Stalin, *Works*, II, 280.
2. V. I. Lenin, *Sochinenia* [Collected Works] (4th ed.; Moscow, 1941–62), XXXV, 58.
3. Y. M. Sverdlov, *Izbrannie Proizvedenia* [Selected Works] (Moscow, 1957–60), I, 268, 276–77.
4. Alliluyeva, *Vospominania*, p. 118.
5. Anatole V. Baikaloff, *I Knew Stalin* (London, 1940), pp. 28–30.
6. Protocols and resolutions of the Bureau of the Central Committee, cited in A. V. Snegov, "Neskolko stranitsi iz istorii partii" [Some Pages from the History of the Party] *Voprosy Istorii KPSS*, No. 2 (1963), p. 19.

7. Stalin, *Works*, III, 7–8.

8. Leon Trotsky, *My Life* (New York, 1930), p. 331.

9. N. N. Sukhanov, *The Russian Revolution, 1917* (New York, 1962), I, 230.

10. Leon Trotsky, *Stalin* (New York, 1946), p. 234.

11. M. Gorky and others (eds.), *The History of the Civil War in the U.S.S.R.*, Vol. II, *The Great Proletarian Revolution* (Moscow, 1946), pp. 187, 294.

12. S. Pestkovsky in *Proletary Revolyutsia*, No. 6 (1930), p. 129.

13. Stalin, *Works*, IV, 122–23.

14. Trotsky, *Stalin*, p. 289.

15. *Ibid.*, p. 297.

CHAPTER IV

1. Trotsky, *Stalin*, p. 357; Trotsky, *My Life*, p. 467.

2. Leon Trotsky, *The Real Situation in Russia* (New York, 1928), pp. 294–95; Leon Trotsky, *The Stalin School of Falsification* (New York, 1937), pp. 66–67.

3. Harrison Salisbury (ed.), *The Soviet Union: The Fifty Years* (New York, 1967), p. 19.

4. Lenin, *Sochinenia*, XXXVI, 554, 558.

5. Nikita Khrushchev's speech to the Twentieth Party Congress (February 24–25, 1956). There are many editions, but I have used the text annotated by Bertram D. Wolfe, *Khrushchev and Stalin's Ghost* (New York, 1957). See pp. 98 and 100 for Lenin's letter.

6. Trotsky, *My Life*, p. 483; Trotsky, *The Stalin School*, p. 69; Trotsky, *Stalin*, p. 361.

7. Stalin, *Works*, VI, 29.

8. Boris Bajanov, *Avec Staline dans le Kremlin* (Paris, 1930), pp. 43–44.

9. Stalin, *Works*, VII, 390.

10. Trotsky, *My Life*, p. 521.

11. Isaac Deutscher, *The Prophet Armed: Trotsky, 1921–1929* (New York, 1959), p. 296.

12. Stalin, *Works*, X, 367.

13. *Ibid.*, XI, 215.

14. Boris Souvarine, *Stalin: A Critical Survey of Bolshevism* (New York, 1939), pp. 482–84. See also Louis Fischer, *Men and Politics* (New York, 1941), p. 98: "Stalin held them by 'special tongs.'"

CHAPTER V

1. Stalin, *Works*, XIII, 40–41.

2. Winston S. Churchill, *The Hinge of Fate* (Boston, 1950), pp. 498–99.

3. John Scott, *Behind the Urals* (Cambridge, Mass., 1942), p. 5.

4. See especially Alexander Orlov, *The Secret History of Stalin's Crimes* (New York, 1953), pp. 314–18; Alexander Barmine, *One Who Survived* (New York, 1945), pp. 263–64; and Elizabeth Lermolov, *Face of a Victim* (New York, 1955), pp. 227–30.

5. Alliluyeva, *Twenty Letters*, pp. 107–109, 112–13.

6. Victor Serge, *Portrait de Staline* (Paris, 1940), p. 95.

7. Stalin, *Works*, XIII, 104.

CHAPTER VI

1. Boris Nikolaevsky, *Power and the Soviet Elite* (New York, 1965), pp. 73, 93.
2. Souvarine, *Stalin*, p. 185.
3. Wolfe, *Khrushchev*, p. 130.
4 Alexander Uralov, *The Reign of Stalin* (London, 1953), pp. 45–46.
5. Wolfe, *Khrushchev*, p. 130.
6. Raymond L. Garthoff, *Soviet Military Doctrine* (Glencoe, Ill., 1953), p. 221.
7. Wolfe, *Khrushchev*, pp. 142, 144, 146.
8. Orlov, *Secret History*, pp. 307–13.
9. Uralov, *Reign of Stalin*, p. 80.
10. Wolfe, *Khrushchev*, p. 158.

CHAPTER VII

1. W. G. Krivitsky, *In Stalin's Secret Service* (New York, 1939), p. 74.
2. Harold R. Isaacs, *The Tragedy of the Chinese Revolution* (Stanford, Calif., 1951), p. 162; Leon Trotsky, *Problems of the Chinese Revolution* (New York, 1932), p. 390.
3. Ypsilon, *Pattern for World Revolution* (Chicago, 1947), p. 165.
4. Robert Coulondre, *De Staline à Hitler* (Paris, 1950), p. 165.
5. *Nazi-Soviet Relations, 1939–1941* (Washington, 1948), p. 75.
6. Gustav Hilger and Alfred G. Meyer, *The Incompatible Allies* (New York, 1953), p. 304.
7. *Nazi-Soviet Relations*, pp. 355–56.

CHAPTER VIII

1. Garthoff, *Soviet Military Doctrine*, p. 187.
2. Generalissimo Stalin, *War Speeches; Orders of the Day* (London, 1945?), pp. 7–12.
3. Garthoff, *Soviet Military Doctrine*, p. 252.
4. 1. V. Stalin, *Sochinenia* [Collected Works], edited by Robert H. McNeal (Stanford, Calif., 1967), II (XV), 35.
5. Milovan Djilas, *Conversations With Stalin* (New York, 1962), p. 38.
6. Averell Harriman, *Peace With Russia?* (New York, 1959), p. 102.
7. Alexander Werth, *Russia at War, 1941–1945* (New York, 1965), p. 410.
8. Djilas, *Conversations With Stalin*, p. 80.
9. Ministry of Foreign Affairs of the U.S.S.R., *Correspondence Between the Chairman of the Council of Ministers of the U.S.S.R. and the Presidents of the U.S.A. and the Prime Ministers of Great Britain During the Great Patriotic War of 1941–1945* (Moscow, 1957), I, 138.
10. Anthony Eden, *Memoirs: The Reckoning* (Boston, 1965), p. 495.
11. Djilas, *Conversations With Stalin*, p. 73.
12. Vladimir Dedijer, *Tito* (New York, 1953), p. 233.
13. Winston S. Churchill, *Triumph and Tragedy* (Boston, 1953), p. 293.
14. Stanislaw Mikolajczyk, *The Rape of Poland* (New York, 1948), pp. 79, 100.
15. Ministry of Foreign Affairs of the U.S.S.R., *Correspondence*, II, 209.
16. Churchill, *Triumph and Tragedy*, p. 636.

CHAPTER IX

1. Stalin, *Sochinenia,* III (XVI), 2, 20.
2. Wolfe, *Khrushchev,* p. 242.
3. *Ibid.,* pp. 214, 216.
4. Marx-Engels-Lenin-Stalin Institute, *KPSS v rezolyutsiakh i resheniakh sezdov, konferentsii i plenumov Ts.K.* [The Communist Party of the Soviet Union in the Resolutions and Decisions of the Congresses, Conferences and Plenums of the Central Committee] (7th ed., Moscow, 1954), III, 384–88.
5. Djilas, *Conversations With Stalin,* pp. 157–58.
6. Alliluyeva, *Twenty Letters,* p. 196.

CHAPTER X

1. Philip E. Mosely, *Face to Face With Russia* (Foreign Policy Association, Headline Series No. 70, 1948), p. 23.
2. Smith, *My Three Years in Moscow,* p. 53.
3. Saul K. Padover, *Experiment in Germany* (New York, 1946), p. 388.
4. Djilas, *Conversations With Stalin,* p. 182.
5. Sir Robert Bruce Lockhart, *My Europe* (London, 1952), p. 125.
6. Royal Institute of International Affairs, *The Soviet-Yugoslav Dispute* (London, 1948), pp. 50, 52.

CHAPTER XI

1. Djilas, *Conversations With Stalin,* pp. 151–53.
2. Alliluyeva, *Twenty Letters,* pp. 196–97.
3. Wolfe, *Khrushchev,* p. 244.
4. Harriman, *Peace With Russia?,* p. 102.
5. Wolfe, *Khrushchev,* pp. 202, 204.
6. K. P. S. Menon, *The Flying Troika* (London, 1963), p. 29.
7. Harriman, *Peace With Russia?,* p. 103.
8. Alliluyeva, *Twenty Letters,* p. 11.
9. Alexandre Metaxes, *Russia Against the Kremlin* (Cleveland, 1957), pp. 53–58.
10. Hutton, *Stalin,* pp. 350–55.

CHAPTER XII

1. Harrison E. Salisbury in the *New York Times,* October 3, 1967.
2. Edward Crankshaw, *Khrushchev: A Career* (New York, 1966), p. 212.
3. Russian Institute, Columbia University, *The Anti-Stalin Campaign and International Communism* (New York, 1956), p. 120.
4. *New York Times,* January 2, 1957.
5. Charlotte Saikowski and Leo Gruliow (eds.), *Current Soviet Policies IV: The Documentary Record of the 22d Congress of the Communist Party of the Soviet Union* (New York, 1962), p. 216.
6. *Pravda,* April 27, 1962.

Bibliography

Few books written about the Soviet Union in the past forty years are irrelevant to the study of Stalin and the Stalin era. The works listed below, though only a minute fraction of the available literature, were chosen as the most significant or representative within the somewhat arbitrary categories that follow. Except for several titles in Russian, only works in English are listed.

1. Stalin's Works

A useful annotated bibliography, arranged chronologically, has been compiled by Robert H. McNeal: *Stalin's Works* (Hoover Institution, Stanford University, 1967). Stalin's *Sochinenia* [Collected Works] (13 vols.; Moscow, 1946–48) is incomplete even for the period up to 1934 that it purports to cover. Nor is it wholly reliable in matters of textual accuracy, for political considerations dictated omissions and alterations. But for his major writings and speeches it is generally adequate. The English translation, which has been used for footnote references, is technically proficient: J. V. Stalin, *Works* (13 vols.; Moscow, 1953–55). Robert H. McNeal, as editor and compiler, has continued the Stalin *Sochinenia* (3 vols.; Hoover Institution, Stanford University, 1967), covering the remainder of his career. Numerous editions of his selected works have appeared, chiefly under the titles *Leninism, Foundations of Leninism,* and *Problems of Leninism.*

2. Works About Stalin

There are over two dozen book-length biographies and many shorter studies. Most were written during Stalin's lifetime and therefore lack historical perspective as well as a full account of his career. Foreign biographies have been generally hostile aside from the Communist and "fellow traveler" variety, while the Stalinist versions are essentially encomiums. The political sensitivity of the topic has thus far barred the post-Stalin generation of Soviet scholars from publication.

Among the serious biographies, Boris Souvarine, *Stalin: A Critical Survey of Bolshevism* (New York, 1939), is a bitter indictment but a pioneering effort that still commands respect. The standard biography is Isaac Deutscher, *Stalin: A Political Biography* (New York, 1949). In 1967 it was updated by an additional chapter but not otherwise altered. Combining literary merit with considerable erudition (and Marxist presuppositions), the book is critical of its protagonist but rather sympathetic to his achievements and consequently out of step with contemporary anti-Stalinist historiography. Leon Trotsky's *Stalin* (new ed.; New York, 1967) was unfinished at the time of the author's assassination in 1940. It is less polemical than one might expect and makes a substantial contribution that only a political opponent with inside knowledge could

[166]

have provided. The relevant chapters of Bertram D. Wolfe, *Three Who Made a Revolution* (rev. ed.; Boston, 1955), probe deeply into Stalin's early career but do not provide a well rounded biography. This more ambitious task has been undertaken by Edward Ellis Smith's *The Young Stalin* (New York, 1967). Although a compelling study of the "underground years," the work is vitiated by the author's *idée fixe* that Stalin was a Tsarist police informer.

The most detailed and up to date biography is Robert Payne, *The Rise and Fall of Stalin* (New York, 1965). Unfortunately (except for those who read for entertainment), it subordinates the historically significant to the picturesque, the sensational, and the personal. Shorter biographies of this genre, though purporting to use confidential sources, are Yves Delbars, *The Real Stalin* (London, 1953), and J. Bernard Hutton, *Stalin—The Miraculous Georgian* (London, 1961). Louis Fischer, *The Life and Death of Stalin* (New York, 1952), is likewise "popular" but a brief and reasonably accurate topical treatment. Henri Barbusse, *Stalin* (New York, 1935), is the least obnoxious of the "party line" biographies.

Among the brief appraisals of Stalin, the interpretive sketch in C. P. Snow's *Variety of Men* (New York, 1967) is sensible and suggestive, and the critique in Edward Hallett Carr's *Socialism in One Country* (part of a larger work; see below, Sec. 4) is fair minded and convincing. The best capsule biography may be found in Robert H. McNeal's *The Bolshevik Tradition: Lenin, Stalin, Khrushchev* (Englewood Cliffs, N. J., 1963). A useful compilation of material about Stalin—mostly snippets from primary sources—is T. H. Rigby (ed.), *Stalin* (Englewood Cliffs, N. J., 1966).

Documentary and other first hand information concerning Stalin—aside from the official record—is scarcer than that for any other ruler in modern times. The Kremlin archives will some day illuminate his political career, but the pre-revolutionary years and much of his personal life is now beyond recovery. The recollections of Stalin's daughter, Svetlana Alliluyeva, despite their political naïveté, furnish the first substantial and reliable information about the dictator's private life: *Twenty Letters to a Friend* (New York, 1967). Another recent work, David Tutaev (ed.), *The Alliluyev Memoirs* (New York, 1968), is an abridged translation of the memoirs of Anna Alliluyeva and Sergei Alliluyev and yields a few intimate glimpses of the young Stalin. Other primary sources are cited in the reference notes of the present volume.

3. The Stalin Era

There are numerous histories of Russia which devote appropriate space to Stalin and his times. General surveys of Soviet history are less plentiful. The best textbook is Donald W. Treadgold, *Twentieth Century Russia* (2nd ed.; Chicago, 1964). George Von Rauch, *A History of Soviet Russia* (5th ed.; New York, 1968), is an objective but essentially somber view, while Ian Grey, *The First Fifty Years: Soviet Russia 1917–67* (New York, 1967), is a lively narrative, less critical in its judgments. Frederick L. Schuman, *Russia Since 1917* (New York, 1957), is sympathetic, fast paced, and rather glib. J. P. Nettl, *The Soviet Achievement* (New York, 1967), is an excellent short history. Francis B. Randall, *Stalin's Russia* (New York, 1965), is more directly pertinent. Although there are few novelties of fact or interpretation, it is a thoughtful, balanced, and occasionally provocative analysis arranged by topic.

4. Government and Politics

Merle Fainsod, *How Russia Is Ruled* (rev. ed.; Cambridge, Mass., 1963), is superior to the many other accounts of the Soviet political system and wider ranging than the title implies. Derek J. R. Scott, *Russian Political Institutions* (3rd ed.; London, 1965), is more compact, though the focus is on the post-Stalin period. The only comprehensive and objective party history is Leonard Schapiro's *The Communist Party of the Soviet Union* (New York, 1960). For the years of Stalin's dictatorship, John A. Armstrong, *The Politics of Totalitarianism* (New York, 1961), a party history from 1934 to 1960, is indispensable to the specialist but hard going for the general reader. For those seeking brevity, John S. Reshetar, *A Concise History of the Communist Party of the Soviet Union* (New York, 1960), is recommended. The dogmatic flavor of Stalinism may be sampled in the official *History of the Communist Party of the Soviet Union (Bolsheviks): Short Course* (New York, 1939).

Stalin's rise to power is recounted with admirable lucidity and dispassion in E. H. Carr's *A History of Soviet Russia* (1917–1929) (New York, 1951–   ), a monumental work of which eight volumes have thus far appeared. Robert V. Daniels, *The Conscience of the Revolution: Communist Opposition in Soviet Russia* (Cambridge, Mass., 1960), while less magisterial and more specialized, offers an impressive guide to the political infighting of the 1920's. Stalin also figures prominently in Isaac Deutscher's masterful three-volume biography of Trotsky, especially Volume II: *The Prophet Unarmed: Trotsky, 1921–1929* (New York, 1959). No comparable studies are available—or seem possible—on the period of Stalin's dictatorship. Selected essays by the late Boris I. Nikolaevsky, long the doyen of Kremlinologists, have been published as *Power and the Soviet Elite* (New York, 1965). Robert Conquest, a worthy successor to Nikolaevsky, has analyzed Stalin's last years (and the politics of his successors) with skill and verve in *Power and Policy in the USSR* (New York, 1961). A more conventional treatment is R. W. Pethybridge, *A History of Postwar Russia* (London, 1966).

5. Society and Economy

Harrison E. Salisbury (ed.), *The Soviet Union: The Fifty Years* (New York, 1967), is a readable and encyclopedic survey by various specialists of the *New York Times*. While oriented to the contemporary scene, it is relevant to the Stalin era. David J. Dallin, *The Real Soviet Russia* (rev. ed.; New Haven, Conn., 1947), a thoroughly hostile interpretation, emphasizes the social order. *How the Soviet System Works* (Cambridge, Mass., 1956) by Raymond A. Bauer, Alex Inkeles, and Clyde Kluckhohn provides insights into Soviet society and the attitude of its citizens. The ablest account of the nationalities question is Walter Kolarz, *Russia and Her Colonies* (London, 1952). Harry Schwartz, *Russia's Soviet Economy* (2nd ed.; New York, 1954), is the best introduction to its subject. A more favorable appraisal (by a Marxist) is Maurice Dobb, *Soviet Economic Development Since 1917* (rev. ed.; New York, 1966). Soviet agriculture still needs its historian, but Naum Jasny's *The Socialized Agriculture of the USSR* (Stanford, Calif., 1949) is a vast compendium of information.

6. Culture and Ideology

There are as yet no comprehensive surveys of either culture or ideology, but various aspects of both topics have attracted much attention. George S. Counts,

The Challenge of Soviet Education (New York, 1957), is perhaps the best general work in its field. A series of essays by Robert C. Tucker, *The Soviet Political Mind* (New York, 1963), deals with both Stalinism and de-Stalinization. Frederick C. Barghoorn, *Soviet Russian Nationalism* (New York, 1956), pioneers a complex and diffuse subject. Postwar cultural vigilantism is documented in George S. Counts and Nucia Lodge, *The Country of the Blind* (Boston, 1949). John S. Curtiss, *The Russian Church and the Soviet State* (Boston, 1953), is scholarly and detached; Walter Kolarz, *Religion in the Soviet Union* (New York, 1961), also covers the non-Orthodox groups. Gleb Struve, *Soviet Russian Literature, 1917–50* (Norman, Okla., 1951), is probably the most useful general work on Soviet literature, while the later depredations of Stalinism are examined in Harold Swayze, *Political Control of Literature in the USSR, 1946–1959* (Cambridge, Mass., 1962). Works of similar scope and competence on science and the arts are lacking. The Soviet propaganda apparatus is discussed in Alex Inkeles, *Public Opinion in the USSR* (Cambridge, Mass., 1962). Herbert Marcuse, *Soviet Marxism* (New York, 1958), is too abstruse for the uninitiated.

7. *Military Affairs; World War II*

Although there is no satisfactory history of the Soviet armed forces, B. H. Liddell Hart (ed.), *The Red Army* (New York, 1956), contains excellent articles by authorities on both military and political matters. John Erickson, *The Soviet High Command: A Military-Political History, 1918–1941* (New York, 1962), while too detailed and technical for the casual reader, is indispensable to the serious student. The best—certainly the most stylistically attractive—military history of the Russo-German conflict is Alan Clark's *Barbarossa* (New York, 1965). Alexander Werth, *Russia at War, 1941–1945* (New York, 1964), is sprawling and uneven but a fascinating account of all aspects of the war. Alexander Dallin, *German Rule in Russia, 1941–1945* (New York, 1957), is scholarly and comprehensive. On wartime diplomacy among the Allies, Herbert Feis, *Churchill-Roosevelt-Stalin* (Princeton, N. J., 1957), is thorough and judicious. The official Soviet history of the war was written under Khrushchev and downgrades Stalin's role, but it is based on archival material: *Istoria velikoi otechestvennoi voiny Sovetskovo Soyuza* [History of the Great Patriotic War of the Soviet Union] (6 vols.; Moscow, 1961–64).

8. *Foreign Affairs*

Robert D. Warth, *Soviet Russia in World Politics* (New York, 1963), a narrative history from 1917 to 1962, devotes proportionate coverage to the Stalin era. George F. Kennan's gracefully written essays, *Russia and the West Under Lenin and Stalin* (Boston, 1961), are severely critical of Stalin's foreign policy. The cold war has found a number of recent historians. David Rees, *The Age of Containment: The Cold War, 1945–1965* (New York, 1967), is a brief introduction. Martin F. Hertz, *Beginnings of the Cold War* (Bloomington, Ind., 1966), is concise and dispassionate; Gar Alperovitz, *Atomic Diplomacy: Hiroshima and Potsdam* (New York, 1965), is "revisionist" history, stressing the political role of the atom bomb. Louis J. Halle's *The Cold War in History* (London, 1967) is an admirable and generally successful attempt to find a middle ground between "revisionism" and the traditional American view of Soviet malevolence. Marshall D. Shulman, *Stalin's Foreign Policy Reappraised* (Cambridge, Mass., 1963), is written in the same spirit though limited to the years 1949–1952. Hugh Seton-Watson, *The East European Revolution* (3rd ed.; New York, 1961), is the ablest account of the "Stalinization" of East Europe.

International Communism, which served as an adjunct to Stalin's foreign policy, has had many investigators of specific Communist movements but few general appraisals. Günther Nollau, *International Communism and World Revolution* (London, 1961), is an adequate guide to the whole subject. Hugh Seton-Watson, *From Lenin to Khrushchev* (New York, 1960), is crammed with facts but sometimes rather superficial. Although dated in some respects, the perceptive interpretation of Franz Borkenau, *World Communism* (new ed.; Ann Arbor, Mich., 1962), first published in 1939, is a minor classic.

Index